The key to preventing
travel trouble is
removing the
opportunity.

This is your key.

The Safe Tourist

Hundreds of Proven Ways to Outsmart Trouble

(and still have a wonderful trip)

by Natalie Windsor
Edited by Rich Lippman

CorkScrew Press
Los Angeles
Distributed by The Globe Pequot Press

Published by CorkScrew Press, Inc.
4470-107 Sunset Boulevard, Suite 234
Los Angeles, California 90027

Distributed by The Globe Pequot Press
P.O. Box 833, Old Saybrook, CT 06475-0833
In Canada: General Publishing, Don Mills, Ontario.

Cover design by Ken Niles, *Ad Infinitum*, Santa Monica, CA.
Cover illustration and ScamWatch! by Joe Azar.

Library of Congress Cataloging-in-Publication Data
Windsor, Natalie
     The safe tourist   hundreds of proven ways to outsmart
  trouble and still have a wonderful trip /
  [by Natalie Windsor]
        p. cm.
     ISBN 0-944042-27-9
     1 Travel—Safety measures.   I. Title.
  G151 W57 1995   910'.2'02—dc20   94-42473

For single-copy orders, call 1-800-243-0495
For quantity discounts, please write to the distributor

Printed in the U S A

10   9   8   7   6   5   4   3   2   1

*For all the good people
who work so hard
to take vacations and
have nice things.*

Introduction

AS YOU TRAVEL ACROSS THE USA, you'll find most Americans to be warm, pleasant and thoughtful. This book will help you avoid the ones who aren't.

Many security and travel professionals have contributed their safety suggestions to reduce your risks away from home. Reading these tips in the comfort of your easy chair or hotel room allows you to mentally rehearse your reactions — so if you're ever confronted by a bad situation, you've already thought out your best response.

You don't have to walk around paranoid — just be prepared. And don't worry about these inside tips falling into the wrong hands; we're just letting the good guys in on the trade secrets bad guys have known for years.

Have a wonderful trip!

—Natalie

P.S. If we've missed anything that experience has taught you, please drop us a note and help us tell everybody.

Thanks to all the experts

WILLIAM L. LONGACRE, Crime Prevention Section, LAPD; **JAMES CYPERT,** Crime Prevention Section, LAPD; **LAURENCE KAUHAAHAA,** Community Police Officer, Maui, Hawaii; **STEVEN D. NYLEN,** Crime Prevention Specialist, LVMPD; **JANICE DaVOLIO,** MD; **CHARLES M. ARONSON,** DPM; **IRVING MEEKER,** DDS; **PALMER R. COOK,** OD; **KATHI TRAVERS,** Director of Exotic Animals & Animal Transport, ASPCA; **WENDY WESTROM,** VMD; **DON LITTLEFIELD,** Staff Director, Member Services, AAA FL/LA/MS; **JOHN PAUL,** Manager of Automotive Technical Services, AAA Massachusetts/New Hampshire; **JAN M. ARMSTRONG,** Executive Vice President, American Car Rental Association; **DONNA ESPOSITO,** First Vice President, National Association of Cruise Only Agencies; **YVONNE NAU,** Disability Specialist, Linli Travel, Tarzana, CA; **ARTHUR LAMPEL,** JD; **DAVE WILLIS,** Executive Director,

AAA Foundation For Traffic Safety; **Cleo Manuel,** National Consumers League; **Rudy Lewis,** President, National Association of Home Based Businesses; **Edward Donoghue,** EAD Associates, Inc., elevator industry consultants; **Bernard Chasman; Marena P. Bennett,** Captain, United Airlines; **Daniel Nemzer,** PhD, Systems Analyst; Robert Murphy, DDS; **Jack Pike & Bev Swann,** Glendale-Crescenta Valley Chapter, American Red Cross; **Madeleine Stoner,** Professor, School of Social Work, USC; **Dennis Jay,** Executive Director, Coalition Against Insurance Fraud; **Julie Reynolds,** Manager of Public Affairs, National Fire Prevention Association; **Centers for Disease Control & Prevention; Ray Ellis, Jr.,** CHTP, Professor, Conrad N. Hilton College of Hotel & Restaurant Management; **Frank Pascual,** Director of Public Information, MTA Bridges & Tunnels; **Peter Shaw-Lawrence,** Society for the Advancement of Travel for the Handicapped; **Dawn Soper,** Public Affairs Officer, Amtrak; **Tim Kelly,** Industry Analyst, Office of Consumer Affairs, Department of Tranportation; **Jane King,** Consumer Markets, MCI Communications Corporation; **Bill Kula,** Public Relations Manager, Greyhound Lines, Inc.; **Debbie Bennett,** Public Relations Manager, ASTA; **Melissa Abernathy,** Manager, Public Affairs, American Express; **Michael O'Brien,** Computer Consultant; **Joe Azar,** World Traveler.

Inside
The Safe Tourist

ScamWatch!™

Pre-Trip Smarts

USA

Before You Leave

☑ Start a **LIST OF THINGS** you want to bring. Write them down *the moment you think of them* so you don't forget (see page 203).

☑ **FORTIFY YOUR HOME** and take steps to make it look occupied while you're away (see page 26).

☑ Be sure your auto, home and medical insurance **WON'T EXPIRE** while you're away. Know what they will — and won't — cover on your trip (see page 36).

☑ **PREPARE AN ITINERARY,** including numbers where you can be reached. Leave a copy with a family member, colleague or neighbor (see page 218).

☑ Carry an **IN CASE OF EMERGENCY CARD** in your wallet, with phone numbers of people to be contacted. Write down numbers for your doctor, dentist, eye doctor and any specialists (see page 216). If you're ever incapacitated, this card will prove to be invaluable.

☑ **MAKE TWO PHOTOCOPIES** of all pages of your airline ticket. Make a list of credit card numbers. Leave a copy with a family member, take the other with you.

☑ Write down the phone numbers of **PEOPLE IN THE CITY YOU'RE VISITING.** Keep this list in your wallet.

☑ Put your **MEDICAL INSURANCE ID** in your wallet.

☑ Call each credit card company's toll-free number to see what **ADDITIONAL INSURANCE AND BENEFITS** come with the card — either free or for a fee. Don't assume last year's benefits are still in place. Ask about medical and legal referrals, emergency transportation, ticket replacement, lost luggage assistance, emergency message service and prescription assistance.

☑ Call your hotel to **INQUIRE ABOUT ITS SECURITY** (see page 164). If you are not comfortable with what they say, cancel and find another hotel.

☑ Ask if **GROUND TRANSPORTATION** to and from the airport is provided by your hotel or car rental agency. Where do you meet the shuttle bus?

☑ Call or write to the **LOCAL VISITOR'S BUREAU,** city tourist office or chamber of commerce for free literature on seasonal events and things to do. Are there any major conventions, sporting events or local holidays at the time you plan to visit?

☑ **DURING PEAK TRAVEL SEASONS** to popular destinations, reserve all your lodging, rental cars, transportation and concert or sports tickets as far in advance as possible.

☑ Double check the **LOCAL TIME** at your destination — daylight savings time, time-zone changes or Indian reservation exemptions can throw you off by an hour in ways you might not foresee.

☑ A light-weight **EMERGENCY ESCAPE SMOKE HOOD** can save your life in an airplane or hotel fire by giving you extra time to escape. Buy one for each member of your party through any travel store or catalog.

☑ A week before you leave, **INSURE AND SHIP BY MAIL** or UPS all items you don't want to carry. If it's going to a hotel, write "hold for guest arrival" on your package. Save the box to ship things back at the end of your trip.

Before You Leave

☑ If you're **BRINGING A BIKE**, pay a local bike shop to pack it up and ship it, insured, to a bike shop near your destination. Have it reassembled on your arrival.

☑ **DON'T RELY ON OLD MAPS.** Get new ones.

☑ **RECONFIRM ALL RESERVATIONS** made by others for you. Call the hotels, airlines and car rental agencies directly. Write down all confirmation numbers, the names of people you speak with, and the times and dates of the calls.

ScamWatch!™
Phony Vacations

THE SETUP

◎ A postcard offers you a trip to Hawaii for 99 bucks IF you call right away. A man on the phone says you've just won the trip of a lifetime; all you have to do is give him your credit card number. A small newspaper ad promises a dream vacation at prices too good to be true — just call a 900 number to find out more.

YOUR BEST DEFENSE

☒ **NEVER GIVE OUT YOUR CREDIT CARD NUMBER** or information about your bank account to strangers on the phone, no matter how tempting the trip or the prize sounds. Instruct your children not to divulge this information, either.

☒ Don't give your credit card number to anyone who calls offering a trip voucher — they often have so many restrictions and conditions, they're useless. **BEWARE WHEN THEY SAY "ALL MAJOR AIRLINES AND HOTELS."** Get specific names. Then confirm with the hotels that rooms for the company have indeed been reserved.

☒ Calling a 900 number to find out what you've won

can **COST YOU $3 A MINUTE — OR MORE**. That's how these companies make money.

☑ Make sure any **"FREE" TRIPS YOU WIN REALLY ARE FREE**. Refuse these offers if you have to buy something.

☑ Beware of offers that **REQUIRE PAYING "PROCESSING FEES"** or "taxes" up front — or "joining a club."

☑ Be wary of **SOLICITORS WHO REQUIRE A LARGE CASH PAYMENT** up front. Take a phone number, check them out, comparison shop and get references.

☑ **NEVER BE AFRAID TO SAY NO**. Be suspicious of high-pressure sales tactics that require a decision on the spot. If you feel pressured, or if they don't answer your questions, hang up.

☑ Ask phone solicitors for a company brochure or written information. **BE SKEPTICAL IF THERE IS NOTHING PRINTED AVAILABLE**, and if they have only a toll-free number or P.O. box. Ask for the caller's name, and ask how they got yours.

☑ Ask if the company **BELONGS TO ANY PROFESSIONAL ASSOCIATIONS**, like the National Tour Association or U.S. Tour Operators Association.

☑ Inquire whether the low-priced trip involves **TIME-**

SHARE OPTIONS. As a trade-off, you may be subjected to high-pressure sales tactics during your vacation.

☑ When dealing with companies you've never heard of, never send any money until you **GET EVERYTHING IN WRITING,** including the *confirmed* departure date.

☑ Be aware that many scam operators book unsuspecting travelers into miserable accommodations, knowing that captive audiences will pay any amount to upgrade to a decent room. **BOOKING THROUGH A KNOWN TRAVEL AGENT IS YOUR BEST DEFENSE.**

☑ **COMPARISON SHOP:** try to match a deal that seems too good to be true with established travel agencies.

☑ Check out any unknown travel operator with the **BETTER BUSINESS BUREAU,** but be aware that scam artists often change their names and locales — no complaints doesn't necessarily mean no problems.

☑ If you've been taken in a travel scam, **DON'T BE EMBARRASSED TO REPORT IT.** If it was a telemarketing scam, contact your city attorney, county district attorney or state attorney general or the National Fraud Information Center: 1-800-876-7060. Mail scam? Take all letters and envelopes to your local postal inspector. Ad scam? Contact the publisher and the city attorney.

Extended Trip?

☑ If you're leaving your car, **CALL YOUR INSURANCE AGENT.** You may be able to cut your premiums by putting your vehicle on "storage" status.

☑ **NOTIFY UTILITIES** if you plan to shut off service.

☑ Check with your local phone company about **FORWARDING YOUR CALLS.** Or make sure your answering machine allows for message retrieval from remote locations. Or arrange for someone else to clear the machine for you, and forward the important messages.

☑ **EMPTY AND DEFROST** the refrigerator and freezer. Set its thermostat to "off" and prop open the door.

☑ If you're leaving your car for a month or more, disconnect the negative (-) cable from the battery. This will help **KEEP THE BATTERY FROM RUNNING DOWN.**

☑ Once a month, the person checking your house should **RUN THE DISHWASHER,** disposal, sink, shower and toilets to keep water in the traps from evaporating and letting sewer gasses into the house.

☑ If leaving during the winter, **DRAIN THE PLUMBING** to protect against freeze-ups. Call your plumber.

Packing Tips

☑ See **THE ULTIMATE PACKING CHECKLIST** on page 203 so you don't forget anything important.

☑ If flying, see page 84 about **LUGGAGE RESTRICTIONS** and items you're not allowed to bring.

☑ **CARRY VALUABLES AND CASH WITH YOU.** Never pack irreplaceable items in checked luggage.

☑ **TEST-DRIVE NEW SUITCASES.** Carry them around the store: are they easy to manage?

☑ You're better off with **TWO MEDIUM SUITCASES** than one massive bag. Even with wheels, you still have to carry it up stairs and over curbs.

☑ Thieves watch for expensive-looking luggage. **CHOOSE BAGS FOR FUNCTION** — leave expensive bags for the owners of private jets.

☑ Many travel thefts involve items taken FROM bags. Thieves "pat down" soft-sided luggage, feeling for goodies before picking the locks. **HARD-SHELL SUITCASES AND LUGGAGE STRAPS** minimize thefts.

☑ **EXAMINE YOUR LUGGAGE** and carry-on bags to make sure they're still sturdy, the zippers still zip and the straps still hold. Do you still have the key?

☑ **ATTACH A LUGGAGE TAG TO EVERY BAG,** including carry-on items, backpacks and kids' busybags. Use your business address — not home — so you don't alert thieves that your house is empty. Use your first initial and last name only on the tags.

☑ Tear off all **OLD DESTINATION TAGS** from your luggage and carry-on bags.

☑ **TAPE A CARD SECURELY INSIDE** each bag with your name, address, phone number and destination.

☑ Give each piece of luggage a **UNIQUE LOOK** — make it easy to spot among the look-alikes. Brightly colored vinyl tape works best.

☑ **DON'T OVERSTUFF** your luggage. Even the sturdiest bags can pop open if they're crammed over-full.

☑ **HEDGE YOUR BET.** Pack at least one complete outfit for each member of your party in each suitcase. That way, you're covered even if a bag is delayed.

☑ If you don't make a written inventory of each bag's contents, **PHOTOGRAPH THE OPEN PACKED BAG** with the first frame of your vacation film. Take a second photo of the outside of the luggage and carry-ons.

These will be useful if your luggage is lost or pilfered.

☑ Count your luggage and carry-on items. **TAKE IN- VENTORY EACH TIME** you leave shuttles, taxis and baggage-claim areas — don't leave anything behind.

The Day Of Your Trip

☑ **REVIEW YOUR MAPS** and brochures — see if you need to acquire any that may be missing.

☑ Have a **BACKUP PLAN** with anyone picking you up in case you arrive late or your flight is delayed. Be sure to have daytime and after-hours phone numbers, and any beeper or cellular numbers with you.

☑ **RECONFIRM ALL YOUR RESERVATIONS** — either directly or through your travel agent. If you'll be arriving late in the day, guarantee your room with a credit card.

☑ Leave the house and car keys, a copy of your itinerary and all instructions with a **NEIGHBOR OR FRIEND**. Be sure these people aren't taking their own vacation while you're away.

☑ **ASSEMBLE YOUR TRAVEL ITEMS** in two separate areas: one for things you plan to check, and the other for things you plan to carry or wear. Keep all your travel papers, tickets and itinerary together.

☑ **LEAVE AT HOME** all keys and credit cards that you won't need on your trip. Stash them in a secure place and remember where you put them.

☑ If you're bringing any magazines to read in the airport before departure, **TEAR OFF ANY ADDRESS LABELS** that show your name and home address.

☑ **FILL A POCKET WITH DOLLAR BILLS** and change for tips and phone calls, so you don't have to open your wallet in public.

☑ Place film in a plastic zipper bag, so it's **EASY TO HAND-CHECK** at the airport X-ray machine.

☑ Check the **WEATHER CONDITIONS** for your route and destination in newspapers, on-line computer services or on The Weather Channel. For more specialized forecasts, call 1-900-WEATHER (the cost is billed to your phone), or 1-800-WEATHER (the cost is billed to your credit card).

☑ **FINAL CHECK:** are the stove, toaster oven and coffee pot turned off? Are all windows closed and locked?

When You Arrive

☑ **CALL FAMILY OR TRUSTED NEIGHBOR** to let them know you arrived safely.

ScamWatch!™
Beware the "Bustout"

THE SETUP

◎ In a bustout scheme, con artists open a travel agency and collect as much money as possible from unwitting travelers before closing shop and heading for the hills.

YOUR BEST DEFENSE

☒ LONGEVITY — how long has the travel agency been in business? Which professional organizations do they belong to? Will they supply you with credible references? Beware of travel agencies that accept only cash, or tell you that you can't leave on your trip for at least two months (the deadline for disputing a credit card charge is 60 days).

Truly Great Travel Agents

☑ FIND A GOOD TRAVEL AGENT the same way you found your dentist: check with friends, colleagues, relatives and frequent travelers.

☑ **QUESTIONS YOU MIGHT ASK:** Are they members of the American Society of Travel Agents or the Association of Retail Travel Agents? Is there a Certified Travel Counselor on staff? Do they quickly access your computer file for your seat preferences, frequent-flyer number, etc.?

☑ How long have they **BEEN IN BUSINESS?** Be alert for constant turnover among employees.

☑ Can you talk to a person on a **24-HOUR TOLL-FREE NUMBER** if there is some travel emergency?

☑ Match your travel agent's **EXPERIENCE AND SPECIALTIES** to your needs. If you're taking a cruise, get a referral to an agent who specializes in cruises.

☑ Does the agency have a computerized **LOW-FARE-CHECK SYSTEM** to hunt for bargains and fare reductions?

☑ Always **ASK WHAT THE PRICE INCLUDES**, and what extras and taxes you may incur.

☑ **GET EVERYTHING IN WRITING** — especially cancellation and refund policies. If you're offered or enticed with a feature or freebie that isn't in the literature, get that in writing, too.

Leaving Home Alone

Fortifying Your Fortress

☑ **TRY TO BREAK INTO** your own home or apartment. Case the outside — by day *and* by night — looking for creative ways to get in. Develop antiburglar solutions — or consult a security specialist or your local police.

☑ Ask local police about a **FREE HOME-SECURITY SURVEY** — and about Operation Identification, which includes etching an ID number onto your valuables, making them tough to pawn and easy to identify.

☑ **INSTALL DEADBOLT LOCKS** on all doors to the out-side, including decks and porches. Make sure the lock has at least a one-inch throw bolt, and the strike plate is anchored in the door jamb with three-inch screws.

☑ **PUT TWO LOCKS** on each entry door. Thieves don't want to pick or break one lock when that's only half the job.

☑ **OUTSIDE HINGES** come off in an instant. Replace them with non-removable pins and secure the hinge plate with headless screws.

☑ **JIMMY-PROOF YOUR DOORS.** Each entry door should be solid wood or reinforced steel, with a reinforced frame. Even then, it can still be pried open if there's more than 1/8" clearance from the frame. Install a latch guard, or have a locksmith install a door reinforcer.

☑ Doors near glass panels should have **DOUBLE-CYLINDER DEADBOLT LOCKS**, which require a key from both sides. Burglars who break in through windows would still have to deal with deadbolts on the way out. If you have only one exit, this type of lock may not be legal; check with police or the fire department.

☑ **SECURE ALL WINDOWS**. Basement, rear bathroom, cellar, skylights and pet doors are often points of entry. Lock and floodlight any areas that are out of your neighbors' view. *Important:* if you can fit your head through any small open space, a burglar can get in.

☑ Many burglars won't attract attention by breaking a window to jimmy a lock. **INSTALL A LOCK OR PEG** that's designed to fit each window. Consider replacing glass panels — especially in doors — with security glass or break-resistant plastic. For more vulnerable areas, consider solid metal bars or grills if they have emergency exit latches on the inside.

☑ Make sure window air conditioning units and fans are securely **BOLTED TO THE FRAME** and cannot be slipped out.

☑ Add key locks and security bars to all **SLIDING-GLASS DOORS** — and place a broomstick in the track. Secure the doors so they can't be lifted out of the frame.

☑ Secure the **WINDOWS ON UPPER FLOORS**. Could a burglar climb a tree to get into your home? Homeowners: lock up your ladders; apartment dwellers: check your fire escape.

☑ **LOCK THE GARAGE** — don't leave your tools lying around to help burglars break into your home. Make sure the door from the garage locks on both sides. Garages offer burglars excellent hiding places and concealed access to your home.

Fortifying Your Fortress

☑ **TURN OFF THE AUTOMATIC GARAGE DOOR OPENER** at the master switch — and lock the garage door.

☑ **CONSIDER AN ALARM SYSTEM**. Have it installed well ahead of your trip — that lets you work out any bugs in the system. Educate a trusted neighbor on how to operate it. If you are concerned about giving out the code, change it upon your return.

☑ You can **ALARM INDIVIDUAL DOORS** and windows, which can be wired to sirens or auto dialers that call police. Motion detectors can similarly be wired to alarms when they detect movement in a house that's supposed to be empty.

☑ Contact only **REPUTABLE ALARM COMPANIES**. Beware of con artists who place phony ads or call households to find out who's NOT alarmed.

☑ **NEVER HIDE YOUR KEY** under the welcome mat, on top of the door jamb or anywhere outside the house.

☑ **INFORM LOCAL POLICE**, your security company and any neighborhood watch programs that you'll be gone, and when you plan to return.

☑ Try to leave a **CAR PARKED AND LOCKED** in your driveway. Or ask a neighbor to park in your driveway while you're gone.

☑ **COVER ALL GARAGE WINDOWS**, so burglars can't see whether your car is there or not.

☑ Use the "Authorization To Hold Mail" form at your post office to get a **FREE VACATION HOLD** on your mail.

☑ **STOP ALL DELIVERIES** and newspapers — but be aware that dishonest deliverymen can pass this information along. Instead, ask a neighbor to take in your deliveries for you, along with any doorknob coupons.

☑ If you stop your newspaper delivery, do it **A DAY OR TWO EARLY,** so you can be certain they've received and acted on your stop order.

☑ KEEP ALL FOLIAGE WELL-TRIMMED around your home to eliminate burglar hiding places.

☑ Create an IN-HOME VAULT. A deadbolt lock and non-removable hinge pins on a solid-core door protect the valuables you leave at home.

☑ MAKE AN ENVELOPE to leave with a trusted neighbor. It should include a house key on a large key ring — NOT labeled with your address — plus your itinerary and emergency phone numbers, and any special watering, feeding, shoveling or raking instructions.

Fortifying your Fortress

☑ Post your neighbor's NAME BY YOUR TELEPHONE— in case of emergency, police will know whom to call.

☑ Use TWO OR THREE TIMERS throughout the house to turn lights on and off; try to match your normal patterns. If you're leaving a cat or dog in the house, use motion sensors so the pet's wanderings trip the lights.

☑ LEAVE YOUR RADIO ON a 24-hour talk station — with the volume high enough to be heard outside the door but low enough not to bother any neighbors.

☑ If you're **TRAVELING DURING THE SUMMER**, plug a window air conditioner into a timer and set just the fan motor to turn on during the day.

☑ If you're **TRAVELING DURING THE WINTER**, have a neighbor leave footprints on your walkways and tire tracks in your driveway.

☑ If you have a **BATHROOM WINDOW**, hook up a multi-setting timer to a light there. That's the room most likely to be used during the night — and burglars notice these things.

☑ Connect floodlights to **MOTION SENSORS** outside your house. For even more security, set the exterior motion sensor to switch on a light *inside* your bedroom.

☑ Arrange for **YARD MAINTENANCE**: lawn mowed, leaves raked, snow shoveled, pool cleaned.

☑ Is your **HOMEOWNER'S OR RENTER'S INSURANCE UP TO DATE?** Have you made a complete inventory of your belongings? See page 43.

☑ Stow valuables in a **SAFE DEPOSIT BOX** with your important papers. Don't try to hide valuables in the house — burglars have more experience finding them than you have hiding them.

☑ Make sure your **ANSWERING MACHINE MESSAGE** says you are away from the phone — NOT out of town. If you don't have a machine, turn down the volume on the ringer so unanswered ringing isn't heard outside your home.

☑ Tell your entire family **NOT TO TALK ABOUT YOUR TRIP** with people outside your immediate circle: hair stylists, handymen, mechanics, etc.

Fortifying your Fortress

☑ **UNPLUG EVERYTHING** nonessential while you're away, especially TVs, stereos and computers. A power surge from an electrical storm could cause serious damage.

☑ Double check your **SMOKE DETECTORS** to make sure they work. Are the batteries fresh?

☑ **LEAVE A FAUCET DRIPPING** lightly to help keep pipes from freezing. Ask your plumber about devices you can check by phone to let you know if the temperature goes below freezing.

☑ Consider asking someone you trust to **HOUSE-SIT** while you're gone. Show this person how to keep your house secure.

☑ Leave **DRAPES AND SHADES** in the front of the house in their normal positions — like when you're home. Ask a neighbor to adjust them when he or she comes in to water your plants. Close the curtains in the back of the house to prevent burglars from looking in.

☑ Don't leave valuables **VISIBLE THROUGH THE WINDOWS.** At Christmas, don't put up the tree in front of the picture window, with presents underneath advertising to burglars. Never leave the tree lit in your absence. Unplug it, even for a daytrip. Keep it watered.

☑ Don't leave the **PORCH LIGHT** on if it will burn all day. Set a timer, or leave it off.

☑ **DON'T PACK YOUR CAR THE NIGHT BEFORE YOU LEAVE** — that puts your valuables in a vulnerable position, exposed outside in a car.

Extended Trip Protection

☑ **PREPAY** mortgages, utilities, loans, insurance and other regular bills that will come due in your absence.

☑ **CHECK THE EXPIRATION DATES** on your driver's license, car registration and credit cards so they won't expire while you're away.

☑ Leave shower stalls and the dishwasher door

slightly ajar to **PREVENT MILDEW BUILDUP.**

☑ If **FREEZING TEMPERATURES** are expected, drain the water system.

Home-Business Protection

☑ **CALL YOUR INSURANCE AGENT** to make sure your policy is up to date and covers your computers.

☑ **BACKUP YOUR COMPUTER FILES.** Put the copies in your safe deposit box with the originals of your important papers and contracts.

☑ Be sure your phone system can hold **UNLIMITED MESSAGES** until you retrieve them from your location.

☑ Put a **FRESH ROLL OF PAPER** in your fax machine — even if the current roll is only half used.

☑ Be sure all your electronic components will reset if the **ELECTRICITY IS INTERRUPTED.** Add a non-interruptible power supply and surge protector.

☑ Consider an **ALARM SYSTEM** that calls for help automatically in a break-in. If your office or equipment is in the garage, secure that area, too. Some motion sensors mount onto your computer — if the equipment is touched or moved, it sets off the alarm.

Insurance Smarts

Ensuring The Best Policy

☑ Your travel agent is not an insurance agent. **CALL YOUR OWN INSURANCE AGENT** before purchasing coverage elsewhere — find out if you're already protected.

☑ Insuring your cruise, trip or tour package is wise if you put down a **HEFTY, NONREFUNDABLE PREPAYMENT,** Combination plans including trip cancellation, default and accident insurance may be offered, but don't pay for any coverage you don't need.

☑ **TO COMPARE POLICIES,** check the deductibles, restrictions and maximum coverage each policy provides. Ask: *"What does this policy NOT cover?"*

☑ **IF YOU HAVE QUESTIONS,** don't be shy about calling the insurance company directly, using the toll-free customer service number on its brochure.

☑ Don't rely on brochures to define coverage — it's **THE WORDS IN THE POLICY** that really count. Take the policy home and read it carefully.

☑ Ask about the **COVERAGE YOUR CREDIT CARDS OFFER.** Pay for tickets, rental cars and lodging with the cards that offer the best benefits in those categories.

☑ **BOOK YOUR TRAVEL INSURANCE** as soon as you

book your trip. Your risk begins as soon as you pay for your tickets.

☑ **CHECK THE EXPIRATION DATES** on your existing policies to make sure none will lapse while you're away.

☑ **DON'T BRING YOUR POLICIES WITH YOU.** Bring photocopies with the insurance company's toll-free number to call if something goes wrong.

Insuring Your Belongings

☑ **"BAGGAGE & PERSONAL EFFECTS" INSURANCE** covers your belongings against loss and damage during travel on airplanes, trains and buses. The carrier will automatically insure your bags up to the amount shown in the small type on the back of your ticket or on the ticket jacket.

☑ You can **BUY ADDITIONAL COVERAGE** from the carrier. Call in advance to ask about rates, limits and exclusions. This coverage is available at the airport or terminal — arrive early to fill out the paperwork.

☑ Determine whether your belongings are covered under your **HOMEOWNER'S OR RENTER'S POLICY** (see "Insuring Your Home," page 43.) If not, your insurance agent can tell you how to upgrade, and whether your policy covers transporting bicycles, etc.

☑ Collecting on a claim is much easier if you can prove what was stolen. Make time to **INVENTORY POSSESSIONS YOU'RE TAKING** before you leave — photos and serial numbers speed the claims process and help you remember what's in your luggage.

☑ You may need a **POLICE REPORT** to verify your loss to the insurance company. After you've reported a theft to the carrier or hotel where it happened, contact local authorities. Get a copy of all reports.

Insuring Your Health

☑ **"HEALTH & ACCIDENT"** coverage provides some protection for emergency medical treatment in case of accident, illness or injury during your trip. This policy can be sold separately, or as part of the trip cancellation insurance package.

☑ First determine if your **PERSONAL HEALTH INSURANCE** covers you outside the U.S., and under non-emergency situations. Know your obligations — if you must call the insurer in a medical emergency, take that phone number with you.

☑ **MANY POLICIES DON'T COVER** activities like hang

gliding, scuba diving and skiing. Read the exclusions carefully.

☑ Make sure your **MEDICAL COVERAGE IS SUFFICIENT** to cover any high-tech, high-cost procedures you could need.

Insuring Your Trip

☑ **"TRIP CANCELLATION & INTERRUPTION"** insurance reimburses you if you must cancel a prepaid cruise or tour because of illness, death in the family or other unexpected events. It can cover you if you miss the departure and must travel to catch up, or if you must return home early. And it can cover an accident or illness while you're traveling.

☑ **READ THE FINE PRINT CAREFULLY.** Are you covered up to the moment of departure, or does it end a few days earlier? Does your policy cover the full cost of returning home unexpectedly from the furthest point of your trip? Does it cover the early return of the whole family if one gets sick? Do preexisting medical conditions matter? Are living expenses covered if you must extend your stay because you're sick or injured?

☑ **COMPARE POLICIES** available through your travel

agent, cruise company or tour operator with coverage available directly from other insurance companies and your insurance agent.

Insuring Against Default

☑ **"DEFAULT/BANKRUPTCY"** insurance reimburses you if the airline, tour operator or other travel supplier defaults or declares bankruptcy.

☑ **DON'T ASSUME** this coverage is included in your trip cancellation policy — ask, and purchase it separately if necessary.

☑ **PAY BY CREDIT CARD** for your trip — if you have problems, you can contest the charge with your credit card company after it appears on your monthly statement.

☑ Avoid **TRAVEL PROVIDERS FACING FINANCIAL DIFFICULTIES** — read the newspapers and check with your travel agent.

Insuring Your Flight

☑ **"TRAVEL ACCIDENT"** OR **"FLIGHT INSURANCE"** covers accidental bodily injuries while riding in, entering or leaving an airplane, boat, train or other carrier.

☑ **PURCHASING YOUR TICKET ON A MAJOR CREDIT CARD** may automatically entitle you to travel accident insurance — you may also be able to buy additional coverage from the credit card company. Call and ask.

☑ Don't confuse the insurance **SOLD AT AIRPORT COUNTERS** and vending machines with any other type of 'travel coverage' — this impulse flight insurance can be very expensive and limited.

Insuring Your Rental Car

☑ **KNOW EXACTLY WHAT YOU WANT** *before* you ar-rive at the car rental counter. Don't ask the counter person to evaluate your personal insurance situation.

☑ If your automobile insurance covers you in a rental car, you probably don't need the optional collision dam-age waiver (CDW or LDW). Before you go, call your insurance agent to **FIND OUT WHAT YOU'RE COVERED FOR.** If you need more protection, purchase a "rider" for your trip.

☑ Many credit card companies offer rental car pro-tection when you use their card to pay. Find out what is covered — and what's NOT. Ask if the coverage is **"PRIMARY" OR "SECONDARY"** — secondary means their coverage augments your own insurance. (You could be caught in the middle while your insurance company and the credit card company haggle over who pays.)

☑ Make sure you have enough **LIABILITY INSURANCE** covering you against others' claims for injury and property damage. It's not included in CDWs and most credit card coverage. If you have your own car insurance, you probably have liability coverage; if not, talk to your insurance agent or purchase it from the rental company.

☑ Before you cross the border, check to be sure your rental car insurance covers you in **CANADA.** No rental companies will allow cars into Mexico.

Insuring Your Home

☑ **"HOMEOWNERS" OR "RENTERS" INSURANCE** covers your personal property against burglary. It's doubly important while you're away on a trip.

☑ **KNOW WHAT YOUR INSURANCE COVERS.** "Full replacement value" gives you full market price to replace your belongings with similar new ones. "Cash value" compensates you at a depreciated rate.

☑ Most policies provide some protection for your

personal property taken from **LOCATIONS OTHER THAN YOUR HOME** — luggage from your rental car, packages from your hotel room, etc. Find out exactly what is and is not covered before you leave.

☑ Check the policy limits on jewelry, computers, cameras, musical instruments, etc. If you need to, **ADD A "FLOATER"** to cover those items.

☑ Prepare a **ROOM-BY-ROOM INVENTORY** of your home, or take photos or a video of your possessions before you leave on your trip. Talk to your insurance agent about the correct procedure. Store your inventory in a secure location off-site, or in a safe-deposit box.

Staying Within The Law

☑ **LAWS AND ENFORCEMENT POLICIES DIFFER** across the U.S. When in doubt, ask a local. One major city may hand out ten jaywalking tickets a year, while another city the same size may ticket tens of thousands.

☑ **NEVER TAKE ILLEGAL DRUGS** from one state to another — no matter how small the quantity. Interstate transportation of drugs is a federal crime with long mandatory prison time.

☑ **DON'T TAKE FIREARMS** across state lines, unless you have verified that possession is legal in each state. If you must transport a firearm, keep it — unloaded — in a locked container in the trunk of your car. If you are transporting a firearm by air, bus or train, ask the carrier about its policies and procedures.

☑ Taking **ANY WEAPON ON BOARD** an airplane is a federal crime. Airline policies vary on what constitutes a weapon — some will confiscate Grandma's scissors from her knitting bag.

☑ **JOKES ABOUT HIJACKING** or bombing are taken very seriously at the airport or on board the plane. Even smart-aleck remarks can get you prosecuted.

☑ All common carriers — everything from planes to buses — have the **RIGHT TO REFUSE BOARDING** or to kick off anyone they believe will be disruptive. Be aware this includes "drunk and disorderly."

☑ If you carry large amounts of cash or travelers checks at the airport, they **CAN BE LEGALLY CONFISCATED** by the Drug Enforcement Administration if they suspect you of drug-related activity. Big sums of cash are automatically suspect. Even if you're released after questioning, the DEA can hold the money as evidence — and you'll have to sue to get it back. Don't carry more cash or travelers checks than you'll need — rely on credit cards and ATM cards, which are easier to protect.

☑ Police officers have **THE RIGHT TO STOP YOU** to ask questions on mere suspicion. Technically, you have the right to refuse to answer, but it is better to give your name and provide identification if requested. You should also answer questions about why you're there. The less attitude, the better.

☑ Remember, any locality may have **SEVERAL DIFFERENT LAW ENFORCEMENT AGENCIES** — such as local police, county sheriff, state police and state highway patrol.

☑ If you're driving a **CAR NOT REGISTERED TO YOU**, have the car's registration and written permission from the car's owner for you to be driving the car.

"Pull Over"

☑ You must always pull over for MARKED police vehicles when they're using **FLASHING LIGHTS AND SIRENS**. Be aware that there is no standard color scheme for police vehicles across the United States. For suggestions on responding to an UNMARKED police vehicle, see page 125.

☑ Use your turn **SIGNAL AND PULL OVER** as soon as speed and safety allow. Pull as far off the road as you can, and don't block traffic.

☑ If there is no safe place to stop, slow down and **SHOW THE OFFICER COOPERATION** by pointing that you're seeking a place to stop ahead. Turn on your emergency flashers.

☑ Unless you are requested to get out of your car, stay seated and roll down your window. **KEEP BOTH HANDS VISIBLE** and high on the steering wheel, until the officer comes to your car. Don't lean down to get anything off the floor or out of the glove compartment.

☑ When asked, take your driver's license and registration out of your wallet and hand it to the officer. Always **TELL THE OFFICER** what you're doing before you reach over to get anything out of the glove compartment, your purse or from under the seat. Avoid any sudden motions.

☑ **BE COURTEOUS.** Answer all questions promptly, and don't argue. Projecting a bad attitude can be very expensive.

☑ A police officer **HAS THE RIGHT TO DETAIN YOU** and your vehicle long enough to check out the registration and license. Standard police procedure requires the officer to inform you why you have been stopped.
Police can also ask you to perform field sobriety tests.

☑ **IF YOU GET A WARNING,** thank the nice officer, look contrite and promise never to do it again.

☑ **IF YOU GET A TICKET** for a moving violation, don't argue — just sign it and fight it in court if you feel it was unfair. If you don't pay it or contest it in court, a warrant may be issued for your arrest. So before you leave the area, call the court clerk to see whether it's possible to fight the ticket by mail.

If You Are Arrested

☑ The officer will tell you what you're charged with. From the moment you're told you're under arrest, you are not free to leave — whether or not they use handcuffs. YOU HAVE THE RIGHT TO ASK whether you are under arrest or whether you are free to leave.

☑ YOU HAVE THE RIGHT TO REMAIN SILENT — USE THAT RIGHT. Do not discuss anything with police until you have talked with an attorney. Give only your real name and address. Go through the booking process politely and deferentially.

☑ If you are taken into custody on suspicion of DRIVING UNDER THE INFLUENCE of alcohol or drugs, you may be asked to take a chemical test. Take the test. In most states, refusing can cost you your license immediately. If your blood-alcohol content tops certain levels on the test, police may also immediately suspend your right to drive.

☑ Most major automobile clubs have agreements with many states for members to use their cards IN LIEU OF CASH BAIL for most traffic offenses — but not all. If you are asked to post bail, see if your auto club membership constitutes bail.

Traveling With Children

☑ You may need to prove you are **LEGALLY ENTITLED** to travel with your child.

☑ **IF ONLY ONE PARENT IS TRAVELING WITH A CHILD,** carry a signed letter from the other parent permitting the travel. Or, carry a certified copy of any court decree that shows you have the right to travel with the child. If the decree is at all ambiguous, have your attorney write a letter stating your right to have the child with you.

☑ **IF ONE PARENT IS DECEASED,** the other may need to show a death certificate to travel with the child.

☑ **IF YOU DO NOT HAVE THE SAME LAST NAME** as your child, you may need to show a photocopy of the birth certificate to prove your relationship.

☑ If your child is **TRAVELING WITH A GRANDPARENT OR NON-PARENT,** the parents should provide a notarized statement allowing the travel. Include a separate notarized statement allowing emergency medical care to be authorized by the accompanying adult.

☑ **TAKING A CHILD ACROSS STATE LINES** without permission of the legal parent or guardian is a federal crime.

Leaving The U.S.

☑ Even a simple daytrip into Canada or Mexico requires proof of citizenship to reenter the United States. **IF YOU ARE A U.S. CITIZEN**, make sure you have positive proof of your citizenship with you. This means a current passport, naturalization or birth certificate, and current ID in the same name as the birth certificate.

☑ **IF YOU ARE NOT A U.S. CITIZEN**, check with the INS *before* leaving the U.S. — prevent any problems coming back in. Not all visas allow reentry. If you have been in the U.S. for several years, your visa may have expired. A change in status or a lapsed work permit may also deny you reentry.

☑ Rules are very strict for traveling with **MINORS INTO MEXICO**. Be sure you have the written permission mentioned in the previous section.

☑ If you're taking a car you don't own into Mexico or Canada, carry the owner's notarized **WRITTEN PERMISSION** that specifically permits border crossings.

☑ Make sure your automobile insurance covers you and your vehicle in Canada. For Mexico, you must **PURCHASE A SEPARATE POLICY** from a Mexican insurance company.

Money
Smarts

USA

Money Self-Defense

☑ **DIVERSIFY YOUR FUNDS.** Carry the bulk of your money in travelers checks. Keep some cash in your pocket, especially small bills and coins for tips and incidentals. Carry one or two credit cards and your ATM card.

☑ Choosing the same number for all your **PIN CODES** will simplify your life. *Caution:* 1-2-3-4, your birthday, your address or Social Security number are not safe choices — pick an obscure number. Don't write the number down anywhere in your wallet, especially not on the backs of your cards. And be sure no one observes or overhears that number when you use it.

☑ Write down or photocopy all the information on both sides of your credit cards and ATM card for a **COMPLETE RECORD** of account and phone numbers to report lost or stolen cards. Keep the copies in a safe place so only you have access to the information.

☑ If you **RUN OUT OF MONEY**, go over your credit card limit, or the ATM swallows your card, a good friend or relative can easily wire funds to you through Western Union (800-325-4176) or American Express (800-926-9400).

Credit Card Smarts

☑ Pay for big-ticket items on your credit card. If goods or services are not delivered as promised, or if the company goes out of business, you can **DISPUTE THE CHARGE** with the card issuer — but only within 60 days of the date on the statement.

☑ Don't take more than **ONE OR TWO CREDIT CARDS** with you on your trip. Remove local department store cards, nonessential library and video membership cards and irreplaceable photos from your wallet before you leave.

☑ **CARD BENEFITS CHANGE!** Call the card's 800 number and check again what the card covers — and doesn't cover — before using it for rental car coverage, baggage insurance, flight insurance, etc.

☑ Check the expiration dates on your cards — make sure none will **LAPSE WHILE YOU'RE AWAY.** Know your credit limit and don't go over it.

☑ Make sure you **GET YOUR CARD BACK** at the end of every transaction — and make sure it's YOUR card.

☑ **DON'T LEAVE YOUR CARD IN PLAIN VIEW** — someone could memorize your card number.

☑ Double check that the **TOTAL ON EACH CHARGE SLIP IS CORRECT** before signing. Take the slip with you to compare with your monthly statement when you return home.

☑ Retail merchants should **NEVER ASK FOR YOUR ADDRESS** and phone number as a condition of accepting your card. The card companies want to know if merchants do this — call the toll free number to report it once you leave the store.

☑ If a merchant still uses carbon paper sales slips, make sure the **CARBONS ARE RIPPED INTO LITTLE PIECES** before you leave the store. Unscrupulous clerks and "Dumpster Divers" can retrieve this information and use your account.

☑ Put your **CARD BACK IN YOUR WALLET** immediately after each transaction — don't leave it loose in your purse or pocket.

☑ **NEVER LEAVE YOUR CREDIT CARDS IN YOUR CAR** or hotel room. Keep them on you. Put them in the hotel safe if you're not using them.

☑ If a child, spouse or parent "borrows" your card — with or without permission — **YOU CAN BE LIABLE** for any purchases they make.

☑ If someone at a gas station offers to fill your tank on his credit card — if you'll give him the cash — don't. He is probably using a **STOLEN CARD,** or a card he "borrowed" from a relative.

☑ **IF YOUR CREDIT CARD IS LOST OR STOLEN,** immediately report it to the card's 800 number. Ask how to get a replacement. Confirm your conversation by certified mail and keep copies of your correspondence. In most cases, you are not responsible for more than $50 in charges per card — but only if you call them within two business days from the moment you discovered it was gone.

☑ If you **FIND A CARD YOU'VE REPORTED LOST** or stolen, don't use it. Call the card's 800 number and inform them it's turned up.

☑ Once you're home, **DOUBLE-CHECK YOUR RECEIPTS** against your monthly statement. Notify your card company by certified mail if any unfamiliar items or mistakes show up. You must do this within 60 days of the date on the statement. You will not be responsible for the amount you are contesting until the matter is settled.

Travelers Check Smarts

☑ Ask about the **SERVICES THAT COME WITH THE TRAVELERS CHECKS:** if they're lost or stolen, how long will it take to get replacements? Are they open on weekends and holidays? Will they give you a cash advance on a personal check? Can they issue you a temporary ID if your wallet is stolen?

☑ When buying travelers checks, **COUNT THEM CAREFULLY** to make sure you've received all you've paid for. Don't leave until you have signed each one in the presence of the cashier.

☑ **RECORD THE SERIAL NUMBERS** and denominations on the receipt. Keep it separate from the checks, and leave an extra copy with someone back home. Keep a written log of when and where you spend each check.

☑ Countersign checks **ONLY WHEN YOU CASH THEM** in the presence of the merchant. Never countersign them ahead of time. If you're traveling with a companion, inquire about one set of travelers checks that can be signed by either person.

☑ **THERE'S NO SUCH THING AS A THIRD-PARTY TRAVELERS CHECK.** Don't countersign travelers checks to someone else — many banks won't honor them.

☑ If your travelers checks are **LOST OR STOLEN**, call the 800 number immediately. Be prepared to tell them how many you used and where. If you're not certain, they will help you determine the accurate amount. You are not liable for anything you didn't spend.

Cash Smarts

☑ **WHENEVER YOU RECEIVE CASH**, put it in your wallet and put your wallet away before going outside.

☑ **DON'T FLASH LARGE BILLS** when making small purchases. Keep ones, fives and tens in a separate pocket, and try to use credit cards or traveler's checks for larger purchases.

☑ Carry only as much cash as you anticipate needing each time you go out. **ATMS CAN PROVIDE EXTRA CASH** if you run short. Be cautious at ATMs — see page 140.

Personal Check Smarts

☑ Don't plan on your personal checks being useful out of town. Before you leave, find out if your auto club, credit card or bank offers **PERSONAL CHECK-CASHING PRIVILEGES.**

☑ Retail merchants should never require a credit card number **AS A CONDITION OF ACCEPTING YOUR PERSONAL CHECK.**

☑ **IF YOUR CHECKBOOK IS STOLEN** — or even one check is gone — report it to your bank immediately. You may have to close your account and open a new one. Make sure your bank still pays all your outstanding legitimate checks.

☑ Don't carry your personal checks together with anything else that **SHOWS YOUR SIGNATURE** — that includes travelers checks, your credit card, ATM card, etc.

☑ If you carry a checkbook, **INSERT A NEW REGISTER PAD** before leaving home. Why reveal your hefty bank balance to prying eyes every time you write a check?

Staying Healthy

Problem Prevention

☑ Always travel with **YOUR OWN FIRST AID KIT** (see page 209). Adapt the kit to each trip — sunscreen to the beach, bug repellent to the campground, etc.

☑ **TIMED-DOSAGE MEDICATION?** Ask your doctor or pharmacist before flying across time zones, so you can compensate for shifting sleep and meal times.

☑ **NEVER** COMBINE MEDICATIONS in the same bottle to save space. Carry a supply that will last *beyond* your expected return date — what if your travel plans change? Bring copies of your prescriptions, too.

☑ Don't pack any medications in luggage where they could be lost — or exposed to extreme heat or cold. Always **CARRY YOUR MEDICATIONS WITH YOU.**

☑ **CARRY SNACKS** with you if you're supposed to take food with your medications.

☑ **TETANUS PROTECTION** needs to be renewed every ten years. Make sure yours is up to date.

☑ Questions about allergies, environmental problems or local epidemics are best answered by a **STATE'S HEALTH DEPARTMENT.** The phone number is usually listed in the capital city of each state.

☑ If you are traveling during flu season, get a **FLU SHOT** at least two weeks before your trip. Flu season in the northern hemisphere usually begins in mid-October through mid-November. A flu shot is not advised if you are pregnant, allergic to eggs, currently have a fever or are ill.

☑ Pace yourself to your fitness level. Do **PRE-TRIP CONDITIONING** before going biking, skiing, hiking, etc. Attention non-athletes over age 35: you're no kid anymore. Consult your doctor.

☑ **DON'T LIFT HEAVY LUGGAGE** immediately after sitting for a long period of time. Take some time to walk around and stretch. Remember to lift using your legs, not your back.

☑ **PREGNANT?** Travel is safest during the second trimester. Get your doctor's permission to travel if you have high blood pressure, diabetes or other medical considerations. Never go to high altitudes, except in a plane, where the cabin is pressurized.

☑ Try calling a **LOCAL PHARMACY** if you need answers about sunburn, first aid, poisoning, drug interactions, to locate a doctor or rent crutches — especially in rural areas.

Food Trouble

☑ **SYMPTOMS OF FOOD POISONING** — nausea, vomiting, abdominal cramps and/or diarrhea — can occur between 6 hours and 3 days after eating contaminated food. Some sources suggest you get medical help if you are not feeling better 5 or 6 hours after the onset of symptoms. But if you can't keep food or fluids down, have a temperature over 100°, dry mouth, dehydration or bloody diarrhea — especially if you are pregnant, elderly or a child — seek emergency medical help immediately.

☑ Always order your **HAMBURGER "WELL DONE,"** so no pink remains inside. If you are served an undercooked hamburger, send it back to be put on the grill again.

☑ Make sure all meats and fowl are **THOROUGHLY COOKED.** If you are served chicken or pork that still has any pink inside, send it back to the kitchen immediately for further cooking.

☑ Avoid restaurant dishes made with **RAW OR UNDERCOOKED, UNPASTEURIZED EGGS.** If you have any question about the safety of Hollandaise sauce or Caesar salad, choose another dish.

☑ Coffee cream can teem with bacteria if left unchilled too long. If the stainless steel container is not cold to the touch, **ASK FOR FRESH CREAM.**

☑ Avoid eating prepared food from **STREET VENDORS AND MOBILE TRUCKS.** They'll be gone long before any symptoms of food poisoning appear.

☑ **ALWAYS WASH YOUR HANDS** — using soap — before eating. Between road grime and bacteria, why risk illness and discomfort on your trip?

Dental Tips

☑ If you have **RECURRING DENTAL PROBLEMS,** pack any appropriate preventive measures and remedies. Your trip isn't a vacation from dental maintenance.

☑ **EXTENDED TRIP?** Visit your dentist at least three weeks before leaving. Consider carrying a toothache emergency kit, available at a pharmacy.

☑ **IF YOU NEED A DENTIST** during your trip, ask the hotel physician for the name of his or her personal dentist. You can also call the local dental association, or a local crown-and-bridge lab in the yellow pages, and ask them to recommend the best local dentist.

☑ If you experience dental discomfort or **PAIN WHILE**

FLYING, the pressure changes could be revealing an underlying root canal problem. Tell your dentist.

☑ If you lose a **CROWN OR PART OF A TOOTH,** let pain be your guide. You can probably wait a few days to see your own dentist if it does not hurt and doesn't look too bad. Do not put the crown back in — bring it to your dentist.

☑**IF YOU LOSE A FILLING,** roll up a small amount of cotton and place it inside the cavity — or try an over-the-counter temporary filling until you can see a dentist.

☑ If a toothache is diagnosed as a **ROOT CANAL** problem, a local dentist can remove the nerve causing the pain. You can then wait until you get home to have the procedure completed by your own dentist.

☑ If you get a **GUM ABSCESS,** rinse with warm salt water and use an over-the-counter topical pain remedy until you can get to a periodontist.

☑ Try not to fly for **3 DAYS AFTER DENTAL DRILLING.**

☑ **IF YOU LOSE A TOOTH,** rinse it off and push it back in immediately — or put it under your tongue or into a glass of milk. *Do not let it dry out.* Call a dentist immediately — your tooth can probably be saved if you get to a dentist or emergency room within 30 minutes.

Eye Protection

☑ Carry your glasses in a **HARD-SHELL CASE** to keep them from getting crushed. Put your phone number with area code inside the case.

☑ Use **REWETTING DROPS** in dry airplane air — even if you don't wear contact lenses.

☑ Carry your **EYE DOCTOR'S PHONE NUMBER**. He or she can often refer you to a qualified doctor, fax you a prescription, or send a new pair of contacts to you.

☑ If you wear contact lenses, carry **FRESH DISINFECT-ING SOLUTION**. Check your travel kit to be sure that the bottle hasn't expired.

☑ If you're not wearing your contacts, **CARRY YOUR LENSES** — along with your spare set. Left in your luggage, they could freeze and become damaged.

☑ **USE ONLY BOTTLED SOLUTIONS** to rinse your contact lenses — not local water.

☑ **KEEP NON-COATED LENSES FROM FOGGING** with a simple trick: after cleaning the lenses, use the corner of a non-lotion bar of soap to mark an 'X' on the front and back of each lens. Then clean gently with a tissue.

☑ In winter, **SET THE CAR HEATER** on "recirculate." Keeping up the humidity level in the car prevents outside air from drying out your eyes and causing sinus problems.

Feet Don't Fail Me Now

☑ Don't break in new shoes on a trip. Bring at least one pair of **COMFORTABLE WALKING SHOES.**

☑ If you have **CORNS OR CALLUSES,** have them trimmed the week before you leave. Or cut a hole in a piece of moleskin and position it around the sore spot — not directly on it.

☑ **PREVENT BLISTERS** by wearing two pairs of thick socks. If you get a heel blister, put a bandage on the blister and moleskin on the part of the shoe rubbing your heel. Never take the skin off a blister: drain it with a pin sterilized by a burning match.

☑ On a plane, **REDUCE SWELLING** by wiggling your toes and rotating your feet at the ankles. Walk the aisles every hour or so.

☑ For **MILD ANKLE SPRAINS,** remember RICE: rest, ice, compression & elevation. Elevate your feet above the level of your heart. If you need crutches to get around, call a local pharmacy. If the ankle is badly swollen or really hurts, see a doctor.

☑ If you get an **INGROWN TOENAIL**, and you can't reach the embedded piece of nail with clippers, soak the foot in warm water and Epsom salts and try again. If not, call a podiatrist.

☑ **IF YOU NEED A FOOT DOCTOR**, get a recommendation from the local podiatric society. Look them up in the yellow pages.

Overdone By The Sun

☑ Everyone — especially kids, toddlers and teens — should **USE SUNSCREEN AND LIPSCREEN** when exposed to strong sunlight. Apply lots of it to all exposed areas before going out, especially from 10 am to 3 pm when rays are strongest. Don't miss any spots.

☑ Use a sunscreen with a **SUN PROTECTIVE FACTOR** (SPF) of 15 or higher. The higher the SPF, the less burning. If you're active, sprays are easiest to apply.

☑ For **MAXIMUM PROTECTION**, apply sunscreen 30 minutes BEFORE going outside. Then reapply every hour or two — especially if you go into the water or perspire excessively.

☑ With regular reapplications, an SPF 30 sunscreen gives you about 300 total minutes of protection (five hours). **REAPPLYING DOESN'T GIVE YOU EXTRA TIME** before you burn — it simply keeps the protection from wearing off.

☑ **SUNSCREENS AREN'T ADDITIVE.** Blending two with SPFs of 10 and 6 won't equal the protection of an SPF 16. It will still give you the protection of an SPF 10.

☑ **WEAR COTTON CLOTHING** that's light-colored and loose-fitting. Shirts with collars help prevent back-of-the-neck sunburn. Wide-brimmed hats cover your scalp and shade your face.

☑ You can get **SUNBURNED THROUGH YOUR CLOTHING.** Most loose-weave shirts only have an SPF of about 8. Wear tighter-weave apparel.

☑ Don't assume your local exposure will protect you from a **PIERCING TROPICAL SUN.** Even indoor tanning booth tans aren't good enough bases — use sunscreen.

☑ Even on **CLOUDY DAYS**, use sunscreen and sunglasses. Overcast skies don't filter the ultraviolet rays that burn you. Sunglasses with ultraviolet (UV) protection will protect your eyes.

☑ **SNEAKY SUNBURNS:** At the beach, sunlight reflecting off water and sand can burn you, even if you're in the shade. In the mountains, unprotected skiers and climbers burn from strong sunlight at higher elevations and the rays reflecting off the snow. On winter cruises, wear sunscreen while out on deck — especially during the first 48 hours.

☑ When **SNORKELING**, wear a tight-weave T-shirt to keep your back from burning through the water.

☑ Some drugs and antibiotics **INTENSIFY THE EFFECTS OF THE SUN.** Ask your doctor or pharmacist.

☑ Don't neglect your pet — **ANIMALS GET SUN-BURNED**, too. See page 81.

Sunburn Relief

☑ Use **"OATMEAL BATH"** over-the-counter products, such as Aveeno, to soothe sunburn pain.

☑ Tannic acid from **WET TEA BAGS** soothes sunburn. Dip a cloth in cool, concentrated tea and gently moisten sunburned skin. If tea isn't available, try cool milk. Aspirin will also help reduce the pain.

☑ **SEE A DOCTOR FOR SEVERE SUNBURN** in case of fever, chills, blistering, nausea or vomiting.

Reducing Jet Lag

☑ You won't feel jet lag flying north or south — just tired. But **JET LAG WILL COMPOUND YOUR FATIGUE** on east-west flights that cross even one time zone.

☑ Skip caffeine the day of your flight, and eat lightly while you're in the air. **DON'T GORGE** on free meals and desserts.

☑ Book your flight so you can **SLEEP ON THE PLANE.**

☑ Alcohol dehydrates the body — **DRINK WATER AND JUICE** instead.

☑ If you want to sleep at an inappropriate time during the day, don't nap — **GO OUT INTO THE SUNLIGHT.**

☑ Set your watch for the same time as your destination city, and **EAT WHEN THE LOCALS EAT.** If it seems early or late to your body, eat lightly.

☑ If you take medicine for chronic conditions, consult your doctor about **ADJUSTING YOUR MEDICATION** and eating schedules.

☑ If you can, **POSTPONE ANY MAJOR DECISIONS** for at least a day after landing — you may not be at your sharpest.

Medical Considerations

☑ If you have allergic reactions, asthma, diabetes, or other medical conditions, wear a **MEDICAL ID BRACELET.** If you have heart problems, carry a copy of your most recent electrocardiogram. Fill out the form on page 216 and keep it with you.

☑ Always **CONSULT YOUR DOCTOR** before your trip. Discuss timing your medications and eating patterns if you'll be crossing time zones. Ask what to do if symptoms worsen during your trip. Ask for a recommendation of a local doctor or clinic at your destination.

☑ **MAKE TWO COPIES** of your prescriptions and a list of your medications, including dosages. Carry one with you; pack the other in your luggage.

☑ **CALL THE AIRLINE IN ADVANCE** and order any special meals. Call to confirm 48 hours before the flight.

☑ **ASTHMATICS:** Request nonsmoking rooms at hotels, and nonsmokers' rental cars. Consider bringing a portable air cleaner and your own pillow, or at least a dustproof pillow cover.

☑ Check with your doctor about special precautions if you are traveling to a **COLD CLIMATE.**

☑ If the air on a plane seems stuffy or hard to breathe, ask the flight attendant to **INCREASE THE FLOW OF FRESH AIR** into the cabin. Try to book a less-crowded flight. If your flight stops en route, don't stay on the plane — that's when the air is the worst.

☑ **HAY FEVER SUFFERERS:** If you know what makes you sneeze, find out what you're facing. Call ahead to the Multi-Data Pollen Forecast Hotline for their free regional pollen report: 1-800-765-5367.

☑ **DIABETICS:** Check with your doctor to see how time zones and climate changes will affect you. Carry an extra prescription for your medication and syringes, since laws vary from state to state.

☑ After a long flight, **TAKE IT EASY**. Test your blood sugar often. Plan your activities so you can schedule your insulin and meals.

Pets In Transit

Before You Leave

☑ Your pet should wear a flat-buckled **ID COLLAR** with its name, your address and phone number. Consider a tattoo ID for your pet.

☑ Make a **VACATION ID TAG** with the phone number of the place you're visiting, or an emergency number where you can be reached on the road.

☑ Take your pet to a veterinarian for a **PRE-TRIP CHECKUP**, a health certificate and documentation of inoculations. Carry it with you.

☑ Pack a **PET BUSY BAG**: food, favorite toys, brush, flea & tick spray and a blanket. Bring the leash with you.

☑ The ASPCA does not recommend **PET TRANQUILIZATION**. Instead, follow the recommendations in this section to reduce your pet's stress.

Pets By Plane

☑ The U.S. Department of Agriculture requires you to obtain a **HEALTH CERTIFICATE** for your pet within 10 days before the flight. Make an appointment with your veterinarian as soon as you know your flight plans.

☑ Make an **AIRLINE RESERVATION FOR YOUR PET**. He must be at least eight weeks old — ask about any other pet restrictions or policies. All airlines limit the number of pets per flight, and domestic airlines now give employees special pet-handling training.

☑ Book a **DIRECT FLIGHT** early in the day, unless you're traveling in hot weather — then fly at night. Try to avoid peak travel seasons. If you have to transfer to another airline, you may have to pick up your pet at the baggage claim area and recheck him onto the connecting flight.

☑ Most airlines allow dogs and cats to travel with you in the plane IF the pet is in a **CARRIER THAT FITS UNDER THE SEAT**. Some airlines charge extra for this. Seeing-eye dogs travel in the cabin at no extra cost.

☑ Most pets travel in pet carriers with the luggage in a ventilated section of the cargo hold. For an extra fee, you can request **PRIORITY COUNTER SERVICE**, where your pet receives counter-to-counter express handling.

☑ You can get **EXTRA INSURANCE COVERAGE** for your pet — request it at the ticket counter when you check him in. Be sure to arrive one hour before flight time to fill out the insurance forms and other standard paperwork.

☑ Get a **USDA-APPROVED PET CARRIER** from the airlines or a pet store. Make sure the carrier has enough room for your pet to stand, sit and change positions comfortably. In big bold letters, label the top and one side "LIVE ANIMAL." Draw large arrows to show which end is up.

☑ **LABEL THE TOP OF THE CARRIER** clearly: your name, contact phone number, the pet's destination, contact name and phone number in destination city, the pet's name, and food and watering instructions.

☑ **ACCUSTOM YOUR PET** to the carrier before the trip. Take your pet for short car rides in the carrier. If you discover your animal has motion sickness, he is not a good candidate for flying.

☑ Never put more than **ONE ANIMAL IN A CARRIER.**

☑ To make your pet's flight more comfortable, place a towel or blanket inside the carrier — it **CUSHIONS AGAINST BUMPS** and turbulence. Carry an extra towel in case your pet has an accident. Put your pet's favorite toy in with him.

☑ If your pet will be flying in the cargo hold, do not travel when the temperature is below 40° or above 80° at either airport. Some airlines may not permit your pet to fly in **EXTREME TEMPERATURES.** Be aware that you may be denied boarding at the gate.

☑ Put **TWO DISHES INSIDE THE CARRIER** — one for food and one for water — and anchor them where they'll be accessible to airline personnel. The night before the trip, fill the water dish and put it in the freezer. The water won't splash in transport, and will melt by the time your pet needs it.

☑ Offer your pet **FOOD AND WATER** four hours before check-in. And exercise your pet before putting him in the carrier.

☑ For **LONG TRIPS** over 12 hours, attach a plastic bag of dry food to the top of the carrier, with feeding instructions for airline personnel.

☑ **DO NOT LOCK** the door of the carrier — secure it so it won't open by itself, but will allow airline personnel to gain access to help your pet in an emergency. Make sure all carrier assembly screws are tightened securely.

☑ **SPEAK UP** if you're told something confusing or see something troubling. Don't be afraid to ask questions. It's YOUR pet.

Pets By Car

☑ **CONDITION YOUR PET** for car travel with a few short trips.

☑ Your pet should be secured during the trip — use a **WELL-VENTILATED PET CARRIER** that's large enough for your pet to stand, turn around and lie down in. Line the bottom with a towel and attach bowls for food and drinking water.

☑ Even though your dog will want to stick his head out the window, he risks permanent damage to his eyes from **FLYING DIRT AND INSECTS**. Bugs can also get stuck in his windpipe.

☑ NEVER leave an **ANIMAL ALONE IN A PARKED CAR.** It literally takes minutes for an animal to develop heatstroke or freeze.

☑ For your pet's sake, if you must travel without air conditioning during **HOT WEATHER**, go in early morning or after sundown.

☑ Always **LEASH YOUR DOG** before opening the car door — no matter how anxious he is. Stop often for stretching and bathroom breaks. Do not let your dog run loose in roadside rest areas.

Pet Lodging

☑ **CALL IN ADVANCE** to make sure your hotel or motel will accommodate your pet. Some charge extra fees, may require a damage deposit, or won't take big dogs.

☑ Ask at the front desk where to walk the dog. Keep him on a leash, and **ALWAYS PICK UP** after your pet.

☑ **DON'T LEAVE YOUR PET ALONE** in the hotel room. You could lose your damage deposit.

Pet Protection

☑ **SOME ANIMALS GET SUNBURNED**, especially pink-skinned dogs, white cats and animals with white-pigmented areas. Apply sunblock to your pet's nose and the tips of his ears — especially in hotter climates.

☑ **CHECK YOUR PET DAILY** for fleas and ticks.

☑ **NOT ALL DOGS CAN SWIM.** Make sure yours can before tossing him in the water.

☑ Upon arrival, keep your pet in a calm, quiet area to give him **TIME TO ADJUST** to his new surroundings.

☑ If your dog starts having stomach problems, give him **BOTTLED WATER** for the first couple of weeks.

Airborne Smarts

Before You Fly

☑ **RECONFIRM YOUR FLIGHT** 24 hours before departure. Call again right before you leave for the airport to be sure your plane is on schedule.

☑ **ARRIVE AT THE AIRPORT** at least one hour before departure — earlier during peak times. Arrive at least two hours before for an international flight.

☑ Wear **NON-RESTRICTING, NATURAL FIBER CLOTHING** and flat leather shoes. Avoid dangling earrings, nylons and hairspray. These can be safety hazards.

☑ If you have a **PRINTED ITINERARY**, keep it in a convenient pocket — refer to it instead of taking out your ticket each time you have a question.

☑ When requesting a seat assignment, the **SAFER SEATS** are generally in the aisle near an emergency exit.

☑ Are your luggage and carry-on bags **LABELED AND PACKED PROPERLY?** (See page 20.)

☑ **TO DISCOURAGE PILFERING,** lock your bag and wrap it in duct tape or a luggage strap before you check it.

☑ Put a **BUSINESS CARD IN EACH BAG** and the pocket of your coat.

☑ Airlines are becoming increasingly strict about **CARRY-ON BAG SIZE REQUIREMENTS**. Call ahead to be sure you won't be forced to check your carry-on bag.

☑ Luggage to be stored **IN THE OVERHEAD BIN** should not have sharp corners. If the bin opens during turbulence, sharp edges are a hazard.

☑ You can check **TWO OR THREE SUITCASES** on flights within the U.S. Call and ask the airline about fees for oversized, overweight and extra bags.

☑ **IT IS ILLEGAL TO CHECK:** matches, lighters, aerosols, spray paint, fireworks, filled scuba tanks, petroleum fuels and many other chemicals. Call the airline or (800) FAA-SURE if you have questions.

☑ Matches and lighters may be carried in your pocket. Do not carry mace, pepper spray or **ANY PRESSURIZED DEFENSE ITEMS.**

☑ Carrying firearms is illegal. Unloaded sporting **WEAPONS AND AMMUNITION CAN BE CHECKED** if they are packed and labeled in a locked, crush-proof container. Call your airline for procedures.

☑ **YOU CAN BE DENIED BOARDING** if you are carrying: any knife, handgun or rifle, mace, assault baton or any of several chemicals. Call the airline for the regulations. Surprise — helium-filled or metallic balloons are not allowed on the plane.

☑ You may be asked to open wrapped gifts or turn on your laptop computer **AT THE SECURITY CHECKPOINT.** Be sure the battery is charged, and have a program available that displays text rather than graphics.

☑ If you are unfamiliar with airline tickets, ask a travel professional to show you how to read them. **EACH PAGE REPRESENTS A DIFFERENT FLIGHT.**

☑ **CHECK YOUR TICKET FOR ACCURACY** — correct any mistakes immediately. Your reservation is not confirmed if you do not have "OK" in the status box on each page of your ticket.

☑ **IF YOU LOSE YOUR TICKET,** call the airline immediately. You'll have to pay for a replacement ticket and fill out a form. Expect to wait 120 days for your refund — IF the ticket has not been used. Having the serial number of the lost ticket can speed your refund.

☑ **NEVER SCUBA DIVE AND FLY** on the same day. Allow at least 24 hours between the two to avoid getting the bends.

At The Airport

☑ If you're parking in the **LONG-TERM LOT**, check your luggage at curbside *before* going to the lot. Park close to the shuttle stop, cashier's booth or under bright lights.

☑ **CHECK YOUR BAGS AT CURBSIDE** to avoid long lines at ticket counters. If you're running late, ask if the bags will be on the same flight as you.

☑ **SECURE OR REMOVE ALL HOOKS** and straps before checking your luggage — your bags can be damaged if they catch on the baggage-handling machinery.

☑ **CHECK THE ROUTING TAGS** on your luggage to make sure they show your final destination. If you don't know the three-letter code, ask. If you check four items, get four claim checks. Protect them — claim checks are your only proof if your luggage is lost.

☑ **BE AT THE GATE** at least 30 minutes before flight time (one hour for international flights). Your advance seat assignment can be released if you haven't checked in one half-hour before scheduled departure — even if you have an advance boarding pass. You can lose your seat to a standby flyer if you haven't checked in at the gate ten minutes before departure, even if you've already checked in at the counter.

☑ **DON'T TUNE OUT** airport announcements — any one of them could affect you. You can even hear them in most restrooms and eateries.

☑ Some airports offer **INTERDENOMINATIONAL CHAPELS,** if you would be more comfortable checking in with you-know-Who before you fly.

☑ Never send your ticket, passport or cash through the X-ray machine — always **KEEP THEM ON YOU.**

☑ If you know certain items will **SET OFF THE METAL DETECTOR,** remove them before the security checkpoint. Place them in your carry-on bag.

☑ Tell checkpoint personnel to keep their **SECURITY WAND** away from your credit cards — their magnetic strips can be scrambled or erased.

☑ **NEVER CARRY A STRANGER'S PACKAGE** — and don't ask strangers to watch your bags.

☑ Make sure the ticket agent tears off **ONLY THE TICKET FOR THAT FLIGHT.** Check to be sure your connecting flight or return weren't also taken by mistake.

☑ Beware of scam artists who create sudden **DISTRACTIONS TO MAKE OFF WITH YOUR BAGS** (see ScamWatch!, page 131).

☑ **AWAKE AND ALERT IS BEST**, but if you must nap, stow your things in a locker. If no lockers are available, use your luggage for a pillow, or keep it between your legs with your arm or leg through the strap of your carry-on bag. Anyone who tries to take your things will wake you up.

ScamWatch!™
The Interception

THE SETUP

◎ While you're busy emptying your pockets and walking through the security checkpoint metal detector, your carry-on bags are sitting unattended at the other end of the X-ray belt. It only takes a second for a thief to grab them.

YOUR BEST DEFENSE

☑ If you're on your own, always watch your things as you comply with the security guard's directions. If you're traveling with a companion, one of you should go completely through the metal detector before the other places any items on the belt. That way, someone is always with your things.

On The Plane

☑ Place carry-on items in an **OVERHEAD BIN ACROSS** THE AISLE — rather than over your head — so you can keep an eye on them.

☑ For faster exits, stow your things in an **OVERHEAD BIN ONE ROW IN FRONT** OF YOU — you'll have fewer passengers in your way.

☑ **OVERHEAD BINS FILL QUICKLY** during winter months. Board sooner if you plan to stow items there.

☑ **SITTING IN AN EXIT ROW INVOLVES RESPONSIBILITIES.** If you don't want them, or plan to drink, ask them to change your seat. *Note:* the seats in front of the exit row don't recline.

☑ Plane designs differ. **LISTEN TO THE SAFETY ANNOUNCEMENT** and familiarize yourself with the life vest and oxygen mask. Check out the safety card in the seat pocket.

☑ **CREATE A MENTAL MAP** of the plane and the two closest exits. Count the rows to both and remember the numbers — it could be dark in an emergency.

☑ **KEEP YOUR SEATBELT BUCKLED** snugly around your hips. You'll be protected from any sudden turbulence.

☑ The air on a plane is very dry. **DRINK LOTS OF WA-TER** and fruit juice — but avoid alcoholic beverages, caffeine and carbonation.

☑ If you ever have to evacuate the plane, **LEAVE YOUR STUFF BEHIND.** It's highly unlikely this will ever happen, but speed is vital. Follow the crew's instructions.

☑ If your plane will be **LATE FOR A TIGHT CONNECTION,** ask the flight attendant to reseat you toward the front of the plane — so you can be first out. Also ask for airport assistance in making the connecting flight or alternate arrangements.

☑ If you **TOOK OFF YOUR SHOES,** begin putting them on again when the captain has announced you're getting ready to land.

☑ On "direct flight" stopovers, if you choose to get off the plane, **ALWAYS TAKE YOUR TICKET** and carry-on bags with you.

☑ **DO NOT OPERATE A CELLULAR PHONE** on or around an aircraft — except with the crew's permission when parked at the gate.

☑ The flight attendants know what they're saying — you must **PUT ON YOUR OWN OXYGEN MASK FIRST** to be in good enough shape to assist your child.

☑ Make it a point to **STAY AWAKE** after the captain announces preparation for landing, so you can swallow frequently to clear your ears.

Landing & After

☑ **BE CAREFUL OPENING THE OVERHEAD BINS.** Items shift during flight, and can tumble onto your head — or someone else's.

☑ **AFTER YOU STAND UP**, check your entire seat area to ensure you have all your belongings.

☑ **GO RIGHT TO BAGGAGE CLAIM.** If you have to make a phone call, use a pay phone in the baggage area.

☑ Stake out a place next to the baggage conveyer and put your carry-on firmly between your two feet. **DON'T LEAVE YOUR CARRY-ON UNATTENDED** while retrieving your luggage.

☑ Bags look alike. **CHECK THE LUGGAGE TAGS** to be sure yours are yours.

☑ **EXAMINE YOUR SUITCASE** — especially the locks — as soon as you pick it up. If you believe someone has tampered with it, or anything is missing, go to the airline baggage claim office IMMEDIATELY and fill out the paperwork before you leave the airport.

☑ **IF YOUR SUITCASE HASN'T COME OUT** when the carousel stops, go immediately to the baggage claim office. Fill out the form, even if they say your luggage should arrive on the next flight. Keep your copy of the form, and write down your claim check numbers, the name of the person who helped you and a direct phone number.

☑ Until your bags are found, some airlines may provide you with a **CASH ADVANCE** — the amount is negotiable. Speak up and ask. Others will reimburse you for reasonable expenses — save your receipts.

☑ If your checked luggage or its contents are **LOST, DAMAGED OR STOLEN,** you can be entitled to compensation. The small print on the back of your ticket outlines the limits and restrictions.

☑ If you **DISCOVER WHILE UNPACKING** that items are missing, call the airline immediately. Take notes on your call, the name of the person you spoke to and what they said or promised. Follow up with a certified letter to the airline.

☑ Don't panic. **MOST BAGS ARE FOUND** within 2 to 48 hours. The airline will usually deliver them to where you're staying — insist if they don't offer.

Buses, Ships & Trains

Before Your Cruise

☑ Ask your travel agent about a SHIP'S AGE AND SAFETY RECORD. Is there a sprinkler system? Do they do safety drills? Under whose flag is the ship registered? How is the crew's English?

☑ If you have SPECIAL MEDICAL NEEDS, ask about the doctor's qualifications. Is the medical equipment you could need on board?

☑ All cruise ships are inspected regularly, and docking at U.S. ports mandates a rigorous U.S. Coast Guard check. Ask about your ship's MOST RECENT COAST GUARD INSPECTION.

☑ The CDC (Centers for Disease Control & Prevention) evaluates and rates each cruise ship's water supply, food preparation methods and cleanliness at least once a year. Ask your travel agent about YOUR SHIP'S SANITATION SCORE before you choose a cruise — scores over 86 are acceptable. Or find out yourself from the Vessel Sanitation Program, 1015 North American Way, #107, Miami FL 33132 or call (305) 536-4307.

☑ If you're prepaying a hefty amount of money, CONSIDER INSURING YOUR TRIP — see page 36. Ask your insurance agent whether your personal medical insurance will still cover you if your ship visits foreign ports.

☑ **BRING YOUR OWN SMALL FIRST AID KIT.** You'll feel better, and may avoid extra fees for visits to the ship's medical facility.

☑ **PACK ALL YOUR PRESCRIPTION MEDICINES,** and bring extra in case your trip home is delayed. Carry your physician's phone number.

☑ **PROOF OF CITIZENSHIP** requirements vary, depending on the ports you visit. Ask your travel agent which documents you'll need to bring with you.

☑ **PREGNANT WOMEN** in their third trimesters shouldn't take cruises.

☑ **EXAMINE YOUR TICKET CAREFULLY.** Make sure it lists everything you've paid for. It also spells out your rights and responsibilities, so read the fine print.

Safety On Board

☑ Pay attention to the **LIFEBOAT SAFETY DRILL.** Ask questions if you don't understand. Know how to get to the lifeboats, and how to wear the life jackets.

☑ Overindulging in food, drink and sun is easy —

especially during **THE FIRST 48 HOURS** of your cruise. Watch yourself.

☑ Don't let a cool sea breeze fool you into thinking you won't get sunburned — even on a winter cruise. **WEAR PLENTY OF SUNSCREEN,** especially during the first few days of your cruise.

☑ Store your airline tickets, passports and other valuables in **THE SHIP'S SAFE.** Don't leave them in the cabin.

☑ Double check to make sure your **CABIN DOOR IS LOCKED** at all times.

☑ Make a mental map of the **LOCATION OF FIRE DOORS** and stairs closest to your cabin.

☑ Use the special fasteners to **SECURE YOUR CLOSET DOORS** — swaying could open the door into your path in the dark.

☑ **NEVER USE THE FIRE SPRINKLERS AS CLOTHES HANGERS.**

☑ If your cabin door requires **A KEY TO LOCK IT FROM THE INSIDE,** leave the key in the door while you're in the cabin. If you need to exit quickly, you won't have to search for the key.

☑ **WATCH OUT FOR SLIPPERY DECKS.** Wear rubber-soled — not crepe — shoes and grip the handrails, especially on stairs. High heels are not recommended on the ship.

☑ Be alert for **RAISED LEDGES IN THE DOORWAYS.**

☑ **NEVER TOSS CIGARETTES** or any smoking materials off the side of the ship — even if you believe they're extinguished. They could wind up inside a vent and cause a fire.

Safety In Port

☑ Attend any meetings to **DISCUSS YOUR PORTS OF CALL.** Listen carefully for any areas they tell you to avoid.

☑ Make arrangements to **TRAVEL IN GROUPS** where street crime is a concern.

☑ Stay in the center of activity — **DON'T WANDER OFF.** And don't be lured away by locals promising "sights most tourists won't see."

☑ **REVIEW CITY SMARTS** (see page 127).

☑ Double check **THE TIME YOU NEED TO RETURN TO THE SHIP.** Wear an inexpensive watch and don't be late.

Bus & Train Smarts

☑ **IF RESERVATIONS ARE REQUIRED,** make them early — especially for peak holiday seasons, weekends and summers.

☑ Make sure your **PRINTED SCHEDULE IS CURRENT** before building other arrangements on your travel.

☑ Smaller stations may not offer porter service. Travel light — **DON'T BRING LUGGAGE YOU CAN'T CARRY** yourself.

☑ **CALL IN ADVANCE** for information on transporting skis, bicycles, musical instruments and golf bags.

☑ If your medication requires refrigeration, **PACK A SMALL COOLER** in your carry-on bag. You may request extra ice if the train has a dining car or at bus stations.

☑ Put **LUGGAGE TAGS ON ALL YOUR BAGS,** even if you don't check them. See page 20 for luggage tips.

☑ Checked baggage is automatically **COVERED AGAINST LOSS AND DAMAGE.** You can also purchase additional coverage. See page 38.

☑ Checked baggage is **NOT ACCESSIBLE** during your trip. On AutoTrain, cars are not accessible either. Carry with you anything you'll need.

☑ Some cities have **MORE THAN ONE TRAIN OR BUS STATION.** Be sure you get on and off at the right one.

☑ In the station, **BE ALERT FOR PICKPOCKETS** and distraction artists (see page 131).

☑ **DON'T BUY A TICKET FROM A STRANGER** — no matter how good the deal.

☑ Double-check you're on the **RIGHT TRAIN OR BUS.** On trains, also double-check that you're on the right car. Not all doors open at all stations.

☑ If you **GET OFF THE BUS OR TRAIN** at an intermediate station, notify the conductor or driver and stay close. Be ready to reboard at a moment's notice.

☑ Sit **CLOSE TO THE MIDDLE** for the smoothest, quietest ride. You'll be farther from the noise of the wheels and the lavatory. Bring ear plugs for extra quiet.

☑ Bring an **INFLATABLE NECK PILLOW** and small blanket in case you get chilly.

☑ **NEVER LEAVE VALUABLES ON YOUR SEAT** — including money or tickets in a coat or jacket pocket — when walking or stretching your legs

☑ **CHECK AROUND YOUR SEAT** and take everything with you as you leave. The carrier is not responsible for personal items and unchecked baggage you leave behind.

☑ A driver's license is not sufficient proof of citizenship when traveling by bus or train between the U.S. and Canada. **YOU MUST HAVE A VALID U.S. PASSPORT.**

Bus Smarts

☑ Don't check luggage in **PAPER OR PLASTIC BAGS.** Ask the driver for the bin number where your bags are stowed.

☑ **TRY TO SIT IN VIEW OF THE DRIVER.** Seats toward the middle of the bus provide the smoothest ride.

☑ Be careful **WALKING INSIDE A MOVING BUS.** Buses are affected by potholes and bumps in the road.

☑ If you are chilly or warm, ask the driver to **ADJUST THE TEMPERATURE** inside the bus. It may be warm up front, but chilly where you're sitting.

☑ **DON'T DISTRACT THE DRIVER.** Keep children quiet and leave home any games that make noise.

☑ If you **GET OFF THE BUS TO STRETCH,** place a note

on your seat to indicate it's taken. Don't leave anything valuable on your seat in a coat or jacket pocket.

☑ **IF YOUR BUS IS DELAYED** and you miss your connection, the bus company should provide alternate transportation, or food and lodging, until they can get you to your destination.

☑ Children 12 and older may **TRAVEL UNACCOMPANIED.** Children 8 to 11 years old must be accompanied by someone 12 or older. Call and ask for information.

Train Smarts

☑ The sleeping compartment **LOCKS ONLY FROM THE INSIDE.** Carry your valuables with you whenever you leave.

☑ Teach your children: **NO RIDING BETWEEN CARS.**

☑ Children between eight and eleven years old may **TRAVEL UNACCOMPANIED,** but only during daylight hours and under certain conditions. Call for information. Children under eight years old may not travel alone.

☑ With 72 hours' notice, Amtrak can provide **ADDITIONAL MENU SELECTIONS** for special dietary needs or disabilities.

Safe Driving

Get Road Ready

☑ Prepare your car wisely — have it checked out by your mechanic. Tell him you're taking a trip and ask him to **CHECK ALL SYSTEMS.**

☑ Do your own **PRE-TRIP CAR CHECK** — see page 120.

☑ **JOIN A NATIONAL MOTOR CLUB** if you're not already covered by any roadside assistance programs. Just one emergency response call pays you back in money and protection.

☑ Check with your auto club, car rental company or hotel about renting a **CELLULAR PHONE.** If you own one, see if your cellular service provider has a "roaming" agreement with your destination city. Or consider an inexpensive CB radio you can use to summon help.

☑ Remove or replace **DEALER LICENSE PLATE FRAMES** on your car before you leave town — they give away that you're a tourist.

☑ **ETCH THE CAR'S GLASS** with the vehicle's identification number (VIN). It's deters thieves who dismantle cars for parts. Check with police for information.

☑ **PHOTOCOPY YOUR LICENSE,** registration and insurance certificate on one sheet — block out your address and add your phone number. Keep a few copies in the glove box. In case of an accident, you'll already have all the paperwork completed, and you can focus on gathering other drivers' information (see page 123.)

☑ Always keep a **DISPOSABLE CAMERA** in the trunk or glove box. If there's an accident, you'll be ready to document the damage and build your case with pictures.

☑ If the car will be driven by more than one person, make sure each driver has the car's **REGISTRATION AND INSURANCE INFORMATION** while he or she is driving — but don't store the papers in the car.

☑ **INSPECT YOUR LUG WRENCH**, jack and spare tire. Make sure they're in good working condition and you know how to use them.

☑ If you're driving from cold weather into warm — or warm into cold — **CHECK THE AIR CONDITIONER AND HEATER** before you leave.

☑ Estimate the combined weight of passengers, luggage and anything you're towing, and don't exceed your **CAR'S MAXIMUM LOAD CAPACITY.**

☑ Car-top carriers make your car more **SUSCEPTIBLE TO HIGH WINDS**. Pack heavier items in the car and trunk. Put lighter things on top.

☑ Never stack heavy items so they're **HIGHER THAN THE TOPS OF SEATS** — loose items fly around inside a car in an accident. Secure what you can, or put loose things — like an empty child safety seat — in the trunk.

☑ If someone in front of you stops suddenly, **STEERING IS USUALLY BETTER THAN BRAKING** for avoiding a rear-end collision.

☑ If you're driving an older car, consider getting a **FUME INDICATOR**, so you don't unknowingly inhale toxic air till you black out.

☑ If you have a car alarm, keep a **FRESH BATTERY FOR THE REMOTE** in your glove box.

☑ **NEVER HIDE A KEY** in or on the car. Thieves will find it. Instead, keep a backup key inside your wallet.

☑ Copy the **CODE NUMBER FROM YOUR CAR KEY**, and keep it unlabeled in your wallet and at home. This enables a locksmith make replacement keys if you're locked out.

☑ **HIDE EXTRA QUARTERS** in the car for tolls, parking meters and phone calls. You can fit 28 quarters into an empty 35mm film canister.

Rules Of The Road

☑ **ALWAYS WEAR YOUR SEATBELT** — both lap and shoulder — even if the car has airbags.

☑ **SAFETY BELT SECRETS:** never wear the shoulder belt under your arm or behind your neck. Straighten out any twisted belts, and tighten them comfortably against your body.

☑ If the lap and shoulder belts are independent, **YOU MUST WEAR BOTH** for them to be fully effective.

☑ Use only **ONE SEATBELT PER PERSON.** Never crowd two or three kids into one seatbelt. Be aware, transporting babies and children without safety car seats is illegal in many places.

☑ Fully reclining the passenger's seatback while the car is in motion makes both the **LAP AND SHOULDER BELTS INEFFECTIVE.** For proper protection, keep the seatback upright.

☑ For safety's sake, **PASSENGERS IN THE REAR SEATS** must buckle up, too.

☑ **SLIDE THE SEAT'S HEADREST** up or down so it's center is level with your ears. This reduces the chance of neck injury in an accident.

☑ Keep your **GAS TANK AT LEAST 1/4 FULL**. Buy gas at self-service pumps during daylight hours only. Pay in amounts that don't require you to go back for change.

☑ **NEVER LEAVE YOUR CAR RUNNING** and never leave your keys in the car — especially to dash into a convenience store or to pay for gas. This is how most cars get stolen.

☑ **IF YOU GET A FLAT TIRE**, slow down and drive to the side of the road or shoulder. If it's in a place that makes you feel uncomfortable, keep driving to the nearest well-lit populated place — even if you ruin the tire and the rim.

☑ Put luggage and **PACKAGES IN THE TRUNK** BEFORE you leave. Stowing packages at your arrival showcases your things to potential thieves.

☑ If you're **LOST OR NEED DIRECTIONS**, ask uniformed police officers; they're your best bet for safety and accuracy. Ask strangers only if you must, and only in well-lit, populated areas.

☑ CB-radio calls for help should never announce you're alone. Say, *"OUR car has broken down. Send a uniformed police officer"* and give your location.

☑ **NEVER OFFER RIDES TO STRANGERS** or hitchhikers — even if they're holding empty gas cans.

☑ **DON'T GET OUT OF YOUR CAR** to help a driver of a disabled vehicle. The best help is to drive to the next phone and report the breakdown and location.

☑ **STRANGERS WHO OFFER TO LEAD YOU** to your destination may not be honest. If you are lost, don't be so grateful for an offer of help that you forget to evaluate its source.

☑ **DON'T BE PROVOKED** by other motorists' gestures or dangerous driving. Never try to one-up a fool or a potential maniac. Put distance between you and trouble.

☑ **IF YOU FEEL THREATENED,** hit the horn in short bursts — not one blast. Also, many auto alarms can be set off by pressing the remote for several seconds. Check the instruction manual.

☑ **ADJUST YOUR BRAKING STYLE** to fit your car — anti-lock brakes work differently. With anti-lock brakes, don't pump the pedal — that prevents them from working correctly.

☑ **TO PARK ON A HILL,** always set your parking brake. For uphill parking, turn your wheels to the left to gently touch the curb on the right side; if there is no curb, turn your wheels to the right. For downhill parking, turn your wheels to the right.

☑ Pulling a trailer improperly can result in **COSTLY REPAIRS AND HAZARDOUS DRIVING SITUATIONS**. Read your owner's manual before hitching a trailer. Legal requirements vary by area — check with local law enforcement before leaving.

☑ **NEVER USE A MATCH** to illuminate anything under the hood — use a flashlight.

☑ Always get specific directions for the **LAST FIVE PERCENT OF YOUR JOURNEY.** You'll be tired and hungry — and more prone to take wrong exits that can leave you lost in undesirable or desolate areas.

☑ **DON'T READ THE MAP WHILE YOU'RE DRIVING.** Pull over to a well-lit, populated area — or have a passenger navigate for you.

☑ **RADAR DETECTORS** are illegal in certain states. Watch for road signs as you enter the state, or check with your auto club.

☑ **KNOW THE COLOR SCHEME OF ROADWAY SIGNS:** red= stop; yellow= caution; orange= construction; green=information;blue=services; brown= recreation.

☑ It's illegal in many places to listen to a **PERSONAL STEREO WHILE DRIVING.** Legal or not, it's a hazard — you may not hear sirens and other vital sounds.

☑ Slow down where you see **ANIMAL WARNING ROADSIDE SIGNS.** Keep your eyes open at night for the reflection of your car's headlights in animals' eyes.

☑ Wherever you are, try to know which way the **FOUR POINTS ON A COMPASS** are facing. You'll make better split-second decisions when you're lost.

☑ Be especially **ALERT DURING HOLIDAY SEASONS** — many more people drive under the influence of alcohol and drugs.

☑ If you are stopped at a **SOBRIETY CHECKPOINT,** you should be detained for less than a minute unless the officer suspects intoxication. In that case, the driver is asked to pull over for a field sobriety test (see page 50).

☑ If you're driving over long open stretches, **CARRY EMERGENCY SUPPLIES** with you (see page 221).

☑ **NEVER TRY TO RACE A TRAIN** to the crossing. The speed and distance of a train are deceptive — it is always moving much faster than it appears.

☑ In national parks, **USE ROADSIDE PULLOUTS TO**

ADMIRE THE SCENERY — never stop on the roadway. Watch for pedestrians, bicyclists, wildlife, fallen rocks and trees — and other drivers not as smart as you.

☑ If the driver starts to experience shortness of breath, headache or fatigue when **DRIVING INTO HIGHER ALTITUDES**, let someone else drive.

☑ If an **INSECT STARTS BUZZING** around in the car, *prioritize!* Your first responsibility is to keep your eyes and concentration on the road.

☑ When **STOPPING FOR A BREAK**, choose a well-lit, populated place. Try to park where you can keep an eye on your car.

Highway Smarts

☑ **INTERSTATE HIGHWAYS AND TOLL ROADS ARE SAFEST** — they're supposed to be regularly patrolled. Avoid two-lane back roads at night.

☑ Keep track of exit numbers, mile markers and landmarks, so you'll **KNOW WHERE YOU ARE** if you need to call for help.

☑ If you've stopped to eat or go shopping or sightseeing — and are uncertain how to get back to the highway — ASK FOR DIRECTIONS **BEFORE** YOU GET BACK INTO THE CAR.

☑ HAVE TOLL MONEY READY in advance. Fishing in your pockets for coins as you enter a crowded toll plaza is very dangerous.

☑ Never get out of your car at a toll plaza. If the tollgate doesn't work, or you need assistance, TAP ON YOUR HORN AND FLASH YOUR LIGHTS.

☑ If you see someone weaving and swerving, or if you pass a spill, accident or debris in the road, TELL THE TOLL-PLAZA ATTENDANT. He or she can call for immediate action.

☑ Be alert for REVERSE-LANE TRAFFIC during rush hour. Signs will tell you which lanes are open in your direction.

☑ Watch for potential hazards FAR AHEAD OF THE CAR IN FRONT OF YOU. Look *through* its windshield. Change lanes if you get behind a vehicle that obscures your vision.

☑ Don't disappear into TRUCKS' OR BUSES' BLIND SPOTS. Don't pace to the left or right of them — the driver won't know you're there. If you can't see the FRONT of the truck or bus, you're in its blind spot.

☑ **IF SOMEONE IS TAILGATING YOU**, slow down — let him go around you.

☑ **SLOW DOWN AT NIGHT** to compensate for darkness and decreased contrasts. Keeping your eyes moving makes it easier to pick out dimly-lit objects.

Staying Awake

☑ Studies show people are wrong when they think they can tell they're about to fall asleep. "Micro-sleep" — a nap that lasts just a few seconds — is enough time to travel the length of a football field at 55 miles per hour. **DON'T DRIVE WHEN YOU'RE TIRED.**

☑ **TAKE BREAKS FROM DRIVING** every two hours — even if you're not sleepy. Stop at a safe, populated area; stretch, breathe deeply, walk around the car.

☑ Stimulants are **NO SUBSTITUTE FOR SLEEP.** But it may help to drink beverages with caffeine, such as coffee, colas or tea.

☑ High-fat foods make you drowsy. **BRING BOTTLED WATER** and high-protein snacks.

☑ If possible, **SHARE THE DRIVING.** If you're a passenger, offer to take the wheel as soon as you notice the driver getting sleepy — or suggest a break.

☑ Some medications — especially cold remedies — can **MAKE YOU DROWSY**. Read the label; don't take them before you drive.

☑ **AVOID ALCOHOL,** especially if you're tired. One drink might not make you drunk — just sleepy.

☑ Wear a **GOOD PAIR OF SUNGLASSES** during the day to reduce eyestrain at night.

☑ Limit your first day's driving if you didn't get a **GOOD NIGHT'S SLEEP**. Respect your body's rhythms, and find lodging during the time you normally sleep.

☑ **CONTRARY TO POPULAR BELIEF,** sleep researchers say that rolling down the window, playing loud music and singing doesn't keep you awake if your body is tired.

☑ **KNOW YOUR SLEEP CUES:** yawning, nodding, unfocused vision and wandering thoughts. Any of these signs are a warning you're about to fall asleep.

☑ Pull over and find a safe, well-traveled place to nap, like a truck stop. Research shows **A BRIEF 20-MINUTE SNOOZE** is very effective — any more than that may make you sluggish.

Highway Breakdowns

☑ **GET OUT OF TRAFFIC** as quickly as possible. If you still have engine power, pull as far as you can onto the shoulder. Turn on your emergency flashers. If there are roadside assistance phones, try to coast along the shoulder to the next one.

☑ **HANG A WHITE RAG** or T-shirt from your window. If you have a "CALL POLICE" sign, put it up. This could discourage opportunists — they can't be sure whether police are already on the way.

☑ **ROLL UP YOUR WINDOWS** and stay in your locked car until police arrive — even if you think it's only a short walk to the exit, or if you have to wait all night. Hide packages and valuables under the seat.

☑ Get out only to **SET FLARES OR REFLECTORS** in case other motorists would have difficulty seeing you. Place flares in a row, about 20 feet apart beginning 100 feet behind your car.

☑ If a **STRANGER STOPS TO OFFER ASSISTANCE**, crack open your window and ask him to call police. Lone women: also say, *"My husband Bruno went to call for help, but I'd appreciate it if you'd call, too."*

☑ If you're an auto club member, ask to see some auto club credentials when a **TOW TRUCK DRIVER PULLS UP** — be sure he's the legitimate help you summoned. If you're unsure, ask the driver to call for police on his radio before you get out.

☑ When it's safe to exit the car, **WATCH FOR OTHER TRAFFIC.** If possible, slide over and exit on the passenger's side.

☑ **IF YOU'RE IN A GROUP, STAY TOGETHER.**

☑ If telling anyone other than police about **SOMEONE ELSE'S BREAKDOWN**, do not mention that the car's occupant is a lone woman.

City Driving Smarts

See also City Parking Smarts — page 151.

☑ **LOCK YOUR DOORS AT ALL TIMES.** In slow traffic or at a red light, your windows should be rolled up high enough so no one can reach in.

☑ Stash purses, briefcases, coats and cameras out of view — even if your windows are rolled up. Be alert for **"SMASH & GRAB"** robbers who shatter windows to get your valuables.

☑ Break the habit of **DRIVING WITH YOUR ARM OUT-**

SIDE THE WINDOW. Or remove watches and rings from the driver's left hand.

☑ At red lights, don't get boxed in. Leave an "escape cushion" of **ONE CAR-LENGTH AHEAD OF YOU,** so you can pull out if you need to.

☑ **DON'T STOP DIRECTLY ALONGSIDE** vehicles in adjacent lanes. If possible, line up half a car-length behind. Keep your car in gear.

☑ **EACH TRAFFIC LANE HAS PROS AND CONS:** the far left lane carries faster traffic, but leaves less maneuvering room. The center lane requires vigilance for cars merging from right and left. The curb lane increases risks from trouble on the sidewalk or shoulders, and it requires greater caution in case of pedestrians or bicycle riders.

☑ **IF YOU'RE LOST,** ask for directions only in well-lit areas, like restaurants or gas stations. Never stop to ask strangers on the street. Uniformed police officers, postal and delivery-service employees have the best knowledge of the area.

☑ **DON'T HONK YOUR HORN** at other drivers. Behavior perfectly acceptable in New York could put you at risk in other cities.

☑ Don't be intimidated by **FREELANCE "WINDOW WASHERS."** If someone comes up to your car to clean the windows, signal 'NO' with your hand.

☑ **NEVER LEAVE YOUR CAR RUNNING** — or leave your keys in the car — when you stop at a self-service station. If you're alone, roll up the windows and lock the doors before going inside to pay.

☑ If you must make a **LEFT TURN AGAINST TRAFFIC,** don't turn the steering wheel until you're ready to go. That way, if you're rear-ended, you won't be pushed into oncoming traffic.

Carjacking

☑ Carjackers look for **EASY TARGETS.** Make it a habit to lock all the doors as soon as you get inside the car. Use your car's ventilation system instead of the windows. Keep your valuables out of sight, even while driving.

☑ **TAKE HIGHWAYS RATHER THAN SURFACE STREETS.**

☑ **IF YOU THINK YOU'RE BEING FOLLOWED,** keep making right-hand turns on well-traveled streets until you find a police or fire station, or a busy well-lit place where you can safely get help. Note the make, model and license number of the vehicle and call police.

☑ **IF A STRANGER STARTS POINTING,** yelling or honking at your car, or telling you something is wrong — DON'T STOP. Drive to a safe, populated area before getting out to check the vehicle.

☑ **IF YOUR CAR GETS BUMPED FROM BEHIND** — DON'T STOP. Motion to the other driver to follow you, and drive to the nearest safe, populated area or police station. If whoever bumped you has criminal intent, it's unlikely they'll follow. Report the incident to police. Be aware if there's injury or damage, you may face a ticket for leaving the scene of an accident — but your safety is worth it.

☑ Be wary if **SOMEONE TRIES TO FLAG YOU DOWN AT AN ACCIDENT SITE.** The best way you can help is to go to a safe area and report the accident.

☑ Decide in advance not to resist **IF YOU'RE EVER CONFRONTED** in a carjacking. Give the thief the car and the keys. Don't fight — stay calm. This is not the time for bravado — your vehicle can be replaced.

☑ Look for **DESCRIPTIVE CHARACTERISTICS** — scars, birthmarks, tattoos. Be prepared to give police the license number and a description of your car.

☑ **DON'T STAY IN THE CAR.** Don't go anywhere with a carjacker if you can help it.

Car Protection Smarts

☑ Thieves look for the **EASIEST TARGETS** — they'll pass up your car if getting in looks difficult. A seasoned burglar can defeat just about any anti-theft device, but send him a message by using any combination of: car alarm, steering-lock device, trunk-lock plate, and ignition or gasoline cut-off switch.

☑ **AN ALARM STICKER** or blinking decoy light could deter an amateur thief — whether or not you have a car alarm.

☑ If you're using a **CAR-TOP CARRIER,** attach it securely with strong fasteners and top-quality locks.

Rental Car Safety

See also Rental Insurance — page 42.

☑ Do not leave the rental counter without a **CLEAR UNDERSTANDING** of how to get to your destination. Write down directions or mark up the map. Ask about any recent problems in the area, and for any recommended alternate route.

☑ For added security, inquire about **RENTING A CEL-LULAR PHONE** — or bring your own from home if your cellular company has a roaming agreement with the areas you're traveling.

☑ If you're arriving late, ask if the rental counter will still be open when you arrive. Or take a taxi to your hotel and **RENT THE CAR IN THE MORNING.**

☑ **READ THE RENTAL AGREEMENT** for where you can and can't take the car.

☑ Make sure no markings, stickers or license frames **IDENTIFY YOUR CAR AS A RENTAL.** Ask whether the rental cars have special licence plate codes. Request a car with an anonymous plate and no markings.

☑ Don't leave telltale **RENTAL COMPANY LITERATURE** on the seats or dashboard.

☑ Request a car with **DRIVER AND PASSENGER AIRBAGS.** Find out which cars are safest — check with the National Highway Traffic Safety Administration or the Consumers Union.

☑ Pack your own **CAR EMERGENCY KIT** for the glove compartment: flashlight, bug spray, sunscreen, maps, brightly colored emergency cloth to tie to antenna, spare eyeglasses, notepaper, pencil, tape, coins.

☑ **TRAVELING WITH KIDS?** Reserve a car seat at the time you make your reservations — or bring your own.

☑ Many rental companies offer a **SNOW BRUSH AND ICE SCRAPER** during winter months. Ask for them, especially if you'll be taking the car to higher elevations.

☑ **INSPECT THE CAR CAREFULLY** for any preexisting damage; make sure it's noted on your rental agreement. Does the odometer reading match the number on your paperwork?

☑ **FAMILIARIZE YOURSELF WITH THE CAR** before leaving the lot. Find the headlights, wipers, dome light, radio, a/c and heater. Take a moment to find the horn. Is there a key release button for the ignition? Which side is the gas tank on? Adjust all mirrors, and find the blind spots.

☑ If your rental car has **ANTI-LOCK BRAKES** — and you're not used to them — remember not to pump the brake pedal to stop, especially in a skid. Instead, apply firm, continuous pressure.

☑ Many accidents happen **PULLING OUT OF THE CAR RENTAL LOT.** Be alert for anything, and keep your eyes open for anyone following you — thieves target these cars, especially at airports.

☑ Tie a ribbon or plastic flower to the antenna, so you can **EASILY FIND YOUR CAR** in crowded lots.

☑ **DON'T DRIVE YOUR RENTAL CAR ON A BEACH** — even if you've rented a four-wheel drive vehicle. The front-wheel drive may have been disconnected and towing charges are very expensive.

☑ The rental agreement also serves as your registration for the vehicle. **NEVER LEAVE IT IN THE CAR.**

☑ **RETURNING THE CAR AT THE AIRPORT?** Check your luggage at curbside *before* taking the car to the lot.

☑ After returning the car, **DON'T TOSS THE RENTAL AGREEMENT IN THE TRASH.** It has too much vital personal information — you don't want Dumpster-Divers to find it. Rip it up.

In Case Of An Accident

☑ Try to **GET YOUR CAR OFF THE ROAD.** Turn off the engine. Don't add to the problem — warn others to stay out of traffic.

☑ **GIVE FIRST AID** to any injured, but don't move them in case of spinal injury. If someone looks injured — but says he is fine — call an ambulance anyway.

☑ If no cellular phone is handy, assign someone to **FIND A PAY PHONE TO CALL POLICE** and request an ambulance if there are injuries.

☑ **WARN ONCOMING VEHICLES**: set flares or reflectors.

☑ No matter what others say — or how much they try to intimidate you — **DON'T ADMIT FAULT** or negligence.

☑ **WRITE DOWN THE NAME**, phone number, address, driver's license number and insurance information from EACH driver involved.

☑ Then collect names, addresses and phone numbers of **PASSENGERS IN THE CARS INVOLVED**, and any witnesses on the street.

☑ **WRITE DOWN THE DETAILS** of the accident while they're fresh in your mind: time of day, weather conditions, speed of the vehicles involved. Draw a map with traffic lights, any construction, one-way streets, etc.

☑ If you have your camera or videocamera, **RECORD THE SCENE** from different angles and photograph the damage to all cars.

☑ **GET A COPY OF THE POLICE REPORT.** Call your insurance company and report the accident.

ScamWatch!™
Police Impersonators

THE SETUP

◎ Crooks sometimes trap tourists by impersonating local law enforcement officers. Be cautious if an unmarked car with flashing lights and/or a siren signals you to pull over.

YOUR BEST DEFENSE

☑ **YOU MUST PULL OVER** — but not right away. Slow down and turn on your emergency flashers. Do not pull over for anyone flashing the brights and honking the horn.

☑ Use a hand-signal to acknowledge, and **DRIVE TO THE FIRST WELL-LIT POPULATED AREA,** like a gas station or convenience store, and pull over there. Often the officer will use a loudspeaker to direct you to a safe place to stop.

☑ When you pull over, your doors should be locked. Officers in unmarked cars almost always wear uniforms. **EXAMINE THE UNIFORM** for a name tag and the correct police patch — not some security guard company.

Open your window only about an inch to talk. A legitimate officer will give the reason for stopping you. If the badge is flashed briefly, ask politely to see it again.

☑ If he tells you to get out of the car, but you are still not convinced, **REQUEST A BACKUP OFFICER IN UNIFORM,** or use a cellular phone to call the police department so you can verify the officer's ID number.

City Smarts

Trust Your Gut

❶ NOTE YOUR SURROUNDINGS. Don't get so caught up in sightseeing or map reading that you ignore what's going on around you.

❷ TRUST YOUR GUT WARNING when approached by strangers, or when you find yourself in an area that seems too quiet, too dark, or full of people just hanging around.

❸ FOCUS ON ANY NEGATIVE FEELINGS — don't ignore them. They're your subconscious giving you a primal advance warning, and you may only have seconds to act. *If a situation feels bad, it probably is.*

❹ IT'S WISE TO TAKE EVASIVE ACTION — suddenly cross the street or do an about-face when you feel unsafe or threatened. Or hop in a cab. Don't sacrifice your safety for good manners. If you take evasive action and you're wrong, no one is hurt.

❺ STAY CALM. Think! Don't be one of the people who say later, *"I shoulda trusted my gut."*

Before Going Out

☑ **TRANSFER THE RISK:** divide your money and credit cards between a fanny pack, several pockets, a hidden money belt — or even your shoes.

☑ **DIVIDE THE RISK:** distribute all the cash, travelers checks and credit cards among the adult members of your group. You'll lose less if a pickpocket gets just one of you.

☑ Carry a **PERSONAL ALARM SIREN OR LOUD WHISTLE** on your keychain — and don't be afraid to use it. Make sure the siren puts out at least 120 decibels of piercing alarm, and always has a full charge. When walking alone, keep it in hand — not buried in your purse or briefcase.

☑ If you carry **MACE OR PEPPER SPRAY**, be sure that local laws don't prohibit it. If you are not proficient with it, or you're hesitant to use it, an assailant can take the canister from you and use it against you. Take a class and learn how to be effective with it. When walking alone, keep it close at hand — not buried in your purse or briefcase.

☑ **A FANNY PACK** tells thieves exactly where you keep your valuables — and can be cut off with a knife. Wear the fanny pack over one hip, so neither the buckle nor your valuables are behind you.

☑ If you wear jeans, **FOLD AND HIDE** large-denomination bills in the little coin pocket on the right front of name-brand jeans. Don't forget that money is in there if you do laundry.

☑ Don't wear jewelry or expensive watches — even fakes and imitations attract the wrong kind of attention. Consider **WEARING GLOVES** over your rings while traveling, or out in strange territory.

☑ Consider substituting an **INEXPENSIVE CAMERA** for your better camera equipment on certain outings. At least keep your cameras and lenses in something that doesn't look like a camera bag — most Army-Navy stores offer a good selection.

☑ Ask your hosts, concierge or hotel manager which **AREAS OF TOWN TO AVOID.** Get good directions and have them mark your map — circle important landmarks and any places you plan to visit. Have them note the locations of police stations. Also, make sure you know how to get back!

☑ Always **CARRY AT LEAST $25 IN CASH** with you. Don't anger a mugger by being empty-handed.

ScamWatch!™
Distraction Games

THE SITUATION

◎ Pickpockets and distraction thieves are very good at what they do. They often work in duos and trios and use a variety of ruses to distract you. They favor airports, train and bus stations, hotel lobbies, elevators, escalators, crowded public places and street corners. You'll never feel them or see them coming. The idea is to divert your attention for a split-second, so an accomplice can pick your pocket or lift your luggage.

THE SETUP

◎ Each of these time-honored setups diverts your attention from your valuables. Many distraction thieves now can be women who target men, or children who target women. They can take advantage of a real distraction — or may have one staged especially for you.

GO ON FULL ALERT THE MOMENT YOU SEE:

☒ The "drunk" who's about to fall to the ground.

☒ Any "fight" that's just broken out.

☒ A stranger who bumps, crowds or jostles you.

☒ Someone in front of you on an escalator who suddenly bends over.

☒ A woman or elderly person who "drops" a suitcase.

☒ A stranger who points out money on the ground or spills a handful of coins.

☒ A stranger who shows you where the roof is leaking.

☒ A stranger who points out a spill, stain or ketchup splotch on your clothes.

☒ A stranger who asks for directions and hands you a map, making you set down what you're carrying.

YOUR BEST DEFENSE

☑ **KEEP YOUR ATTENTION ON YOUR SITUATION — NOT ON THE DISTRACTION.** Don't stop and DO NOT put down your bags or luggage — keep moving.

☑ Men should wear their wallets in a front pocket or inside jacket pocket — never the back pocket. **USE MONEYBELTS,** hidden travel wallets or sew an inner pocket into your clothes.

☑ Make a conscious deliberate effort not to show pickpockets where you keep your money. **KEEP SEVERAL SMALL BILLS IN YOUR POCKET** so you don't have to take out your wallet in crowded places. And be aware of any giveaway signals you could show, such as unconsciously tapping the place you keep your valuables.

☑ If you suspect you have been bumped intentionally, this could be a warning that **AN ACCOMPLICE MAY BE READY TO STEAL** any of your exposed belongings.

☑ If you suspect your pocket has been picked, **MAKE A SCENE** and shout, *"That guy got my wallet, somebody get him."* Pickpockets hate to be noticed.

On The Streets

☑ It's **RISKY TO WALK ALONE** — solo pedestrians are the biggest targets. Find others to accompany you — even for short distances.

☑ Walk with a **SENSE OF PURPOSE** and a confident stride. Even if you're lost, try not to look unsure.

☑ **IF YOU ARE ALONE,** and must walk past anything that makes you nervous, remember you can wait for others to walk by and quietly tag along with the group. Or take a detour down a well-lit, main boulevard —

even if you have to walk a few extra blocks.

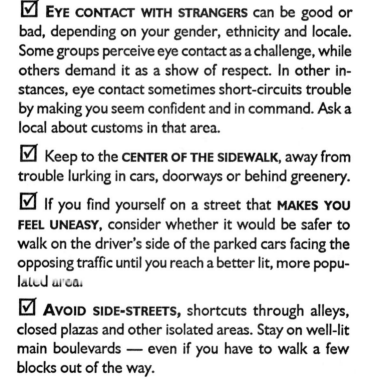

☑ Don't just look straight ahead. Turn your head and **SCAN THE SCENE** around you from time to time.

☑ If you need a **SAFE PLACE TO REST**, try a coffee shop, hotel lobby or a church.

☑ **EYE CONTACT WITH STRANGERS** can be good or bad, depending on your gender, ethnicity and locale. Some groups perceive eye contact as a challenge, while others demand it as a show of respect. In other instances, eye contact sometimes short-circuits trouble by making you seem confident and in command. Ask a local about customs in that area.

☑ Keep to the **CENTER OF THE SIDEWALK**, away from trouble lurking in cars, doorways or behind greenery.

☑ If you find yourself on a street that **MAKES YOU FEEL UNEASY**, consider whether it would be safer to walk on the driver's side of the parked cars facing the opposing traffic until you reach a better lit, more populated area.

☑ **AVOID SIDE-STREETS,** shortcuts through alleys, closed plazas and other isolated areas. Stay on well-lit main boulevards — even if you have to walk a few blocks out of the way.

☑ Find **AN INCONSPICUOUS PLACE** to consult a map — don't be conspicuously unsure. Even better, know where you're headed before you go out.

☑ **STAY ALERT.** Daydreaming or window shopping makes you a prime target.

☑ **MAKE SPECIFIC PLANS** to rendezvous with friends. *"Meet us in front,"* is not as clear as, *"The southwest corner under the red awning."*

☑ **JOGGING TRIP-UPS:** don't jog in unfamiliar areas, and avoid isolated parks and paths. Jog without anything that will take your attention away from your surroundings, such as a stereo headset. Jog with a partner and don't run to exhaustion. Carry a pocket siren. Run against the flow of traffic. Carry ID and enough coins to make a phone call. Don't wear anything too provocative, or baggy enough to be easily grabbed.

☑ Women: see **PURSE SMARTS**, page 185.

☑ Carrying **TOO MANY SHOPPING BAGS** and packages makes you an easy target. Better to call a cab.

☑ No matter how nice he looks, **DON'T LET A STRANGER** carry your luggage.

☑ If your route gives you an uneasy feeling, call for a **TAXI AT NIGHT** — even if your destination is within walking distance.

☑ **WHEN ARRIVING IN A NEW CITY**, do not wander around outside the bus or train terminal — it may not be in the best part of town. Stay inside near security guards until you know where you're going.

☑ **BE WARY OF STRANGERS** who want to talk to you or ask for directions or the time. Don't stop — keep walking and try to keep a six-foot distance between you. Announce loudly, *"My brother's waiting for me — he gets angry when I'm late."* Your best bet is to be very loud and to keep walking.

☑ Don't even stop to watch **ILLEGAL STREET GAMES** set up on cardboard boxes — they're rigged so you can't win, and pickpockets often work the crowd. "Winners" are often nicely dressed shills — others are often followed and mugged.

☑ Avoid **SOLITARY STREET VENDORS**. You don't really believe that's a Rolex for 35 bucks, do you?

☑ Be cautious if a stranger makes any request that means **YOU'LL HAVE TO TAKE OUT YOUR WALLET** — no matter how urgent the reason. If you're asked to make change for a $20 or $50 dollar bill on the street, suggest that person go to a bank or store.

☑ **IF A STRANGER MUTTERS** at you as you pass, keep walking. It's either a proposition you don't want to hear, or an offer to sell you drugs. Either way, you'll be at risk. (By the way, any drugs sold on the street are likely to be sugar or oregano.)

☑ Stay in highly populated areas of **CITY PARKS** — don't walk down lonely paths or explore hidden areas, especially at night. Go with a group rather than by yourself.

☑ If you think **YOU'RE BEING FOLLOWED:**

❶ Glance back to acknowledge you know he's there.

❷ Cross the street.

❸ Run into a store or restaurant. Call a taxi or a friend to pick you up — or call the police. Do not stop to call for help at a pay phone on the street.

❹ If there's no store open, wave at a nearby person and shout, *"Hey, you dropped something."* You can then explain your situation and ask if she'll walk you to a phone so you can call the police.

ScamWatch!™
Shoulder Surfers

THE SITUATION

◎ Eagle-eyed thieves — some with binoculars — get your long-distance phone card number by watching you tap it in at pay phones or overhearing you say it. These "shoulder surfers" then peddle time on your card to others on the street. Hundreds of dollars' worth of calls can suddenly turn up on your phone bill to places you've never even heard of.

THE SETUP

☒ People loitering around the phone you're using, watching or listening to you place your call.

☒ Open phone kiosks in airports and port authority terminals.

☒ Careless callers — more than with any other scam, you control your vulnerability.

YOUR BEST DEFENSE

☑ MEMORIZE YOUR PHONE-CARD NUMBER before leaving on your trip.

☑ When dialing in public, **STAND CLOSE TO THE PHONE.** Hold one hand over the other as you dial. When possible, insert your calling card into phones that accept it. Don't hold up your card for others to see. Speak in a quiet voice if you need to say your number to an operator.

☑ If people are loitering, **GO TO A DIFFERENT PHONE** and wait until no one's around.

☑ If you plan to start using your card heavily or alter your calling patterns significantly, **ALERT YOUR LONG-DISTANCE COMPANY** before you leave so they won't shut off your card in mid-trip, when their computers detect the change in card usage.

☑ You are not responsible for fraudulent calls made on your card — **CALL YOUR LONG DISTANCE COMPANY** the instant you realize your card is stolen, or suspect the number could have been lifted — so they can issue you an alternate calling card number. If they detect the theft first, and shut off your card, most long distance companies will try to alert you by calling your home or office.

☑ You ARE responsible for **CALLS MADE BY MEMBERS OF YOUR FAMILY,** so treat your calling card the way you treat your credit card.

Pay Phone Protocol

☑ Never use pay phones that are not in a **WELL-LIT, POPULATED AREA.** If the location of one pay phone makes you uncomfortable, look for another in a restaurant or building lobby. If you notice all the pay phones on a particular street are vandalized, don't linger in that area.

☑ While at a pay phone, turn your back to the phone and **FACE OUTWARD.** You're more vulnerable with your back to your surroundings.

☑ **DON'T PUT DOWN** your wallet, keys or credit cards by the phone. Keep your luggage on the ground between your legs, and hold onto your purse.

☑ If you are with a companion, have this person **BE A CONSPICUOUS LOOKOUT** in the car or across the street. Your protection is greater with a wider field of vision and more options to make noise or get help.

ATM Safety

☑ Keep your ATM card in a **SAFE PLACE.** If it's lost or stolen, call your bank immediately. Your liability rises after just two business days.

☑ **GOOD ATMs**: Inside supermarkets and convenience stores, where it's well-lit and busy.

☒ **RISKY ATMs:** Any isolated location, near shrubbery or alleyways, and at night.

☑ At the ATM, **IF ANYTHING MAKES YOU UNCOMFORTABLE,** push the 'CANCEL' button, take your card and leave.

☑ Don't assume that a person standing at the ATM when you arrive is using it legitimately — he could be **WAITING FOR A VICTIM.** Wait till he leaves before using the ATM, or go elsewhere.

☑ Some institutions are installing wide-angle mirrors for rear vision at their ATMs. If yours doesn't have this, use the plexiglass to **WATCH REFLECTIONS** behind you.

☑ A companion can **BE A BETTER LOOKOUT** by waiting in the car or across the street — rather than standing next to you.

☑ **MINIMIZE YOUR EXPOSURE.** Put cash away quickly and count it later. Never leave your receipt.

☑ Choose an ATM with limited access and **CLEAR SIGHTLINES.** Cash dispensers on corners or next to driveways or alleys give crooks an advantage.

☑ Always **SHIELD YOUR NUMBER** from prying eyes as you punch it in. Don't drop your guard, even at grocery stores and gas stations.

☑ At the end of your transaction, make sure you **TAKE YOUR CARD** with you.

☑ If you're approached by a stranger or feel you're being followed after completing an ATM transaction, **SLIP INTO A RESTAURANT** or store until you feel the coast is clear.

☑ **THE BEST DEFENSE IS PREVENTION.** If confronted by an attacker, hand over the money. Guaranteed, your safety is worth more.

Drive-Up ATMs

☑ **SCOPE OUT THE ATM** before pulling into the driveway — a 90-second trip around the block is surprisingly effective protection.

☑ **KEEP YOUR CAR DOORS LOCKED** and windows closed. Put the car in park but keep the engine running.

☑ **IF ANYONE APPROACHES YOUR CAR** in a way that makes you nervous, hit the 'CANCEL' button and hit your horn in short staccato bursts.

ScamWatch!™
ATM Spies

THE SITUATION

◎ Crooks use videocameras positioned in nearby vans or campers to capture your PIN number on tape. After one of them picks up your discarded receipt, they use a laptop computer and card programmer to create a bogus ATM card — then they start emptying your account. The theft is often not discovered until your monthly statement arrives.

YOUR BEST DEFENSE

☑ **STAND CLOSE, DIRECTLY IN FRONT OF THE ATM,** and shield the keypad as you enter your secret code. This scam works only if you leave your receipt. Always take your receipt with you.

Elevator Safety

☑ Don't get onto an elevator with anyone who makes you feel **UNSAFE OR UNCOMFORTABLE.** Say, *"Oops...I left my book on the chair."* and leave. Take the next car or wait for the elevator to return empty.

☑ Anyone who doesn't press his own button is planning to get off on your floor. **IF THIS MAKES YOU UNCOMFORTABLE**, press the lobby button and say, *"Oops...I forgot my sunglasses."* Then return to the lobby before going back to your floor.

☑ If you're alone, never stay on an elevator **HEADED FOR THE BASEMENT.**

☑ If you aren't sure which floor is on **STREET LEVEL**, press the button with the '☆' symbol.

☑ Check to make sure the elevator is **LEVEL WITH THE FLOOR** before entering or exiting, especially if you're carrying packages or luggage.

☑ **NEVER TRY TO CATCH** an elevator that's leaving by sticking your hand into the doors. The safety edge that opens the doors becomes non-operational just as the doors shut. Press the button in the hall instead.

☑ If your elevator gets **STUCK BETWEEN FLOORS**, press the alarm button. Never try to get out on your own. Safety mechanisms will not allow the elevator to fall. You're more likely to get hurt if you try to climb out.

☑ You're safer in newer elevators — the **'STOP' BUTTON HAS BEEN ELIMINATED.** Strangers can no longer stop an elevator between floors.

Restroom Reconnaissance

☑ It's best to use a safe, available restroom **BEFORE YOU LEAVE** familiar surroundings.

☑ The most available restrooms are in buildings that deal in service: upscale **DEPARTMENT STORES AND HOTELS**. However, these are not guarded, so be aware that anyone from the street can be in there with you.

☑ Some establishments still have **PAY TOILETS**, though many provide tokens to their customers. Carry change with you, and be aware that pay toilets are often favorite waiting places for trouble.

☑ **OFFICE BUILDINGS** often lock their restrooms, but every business on the floor should have a key. In an emergency, ask a receptionist.

☑ **RESTAURANTS** may require you to be a customer, but you can order a soft drink to go and ask them to prepare it for you while you use the restroom.

☑ In most businesses, **ASK THE HELP** if you may use the employees' restroom. Even grocery stores are required to have facilities, though not required to advertise them.

☑ **RESTROOMS TO AVOID**: transit stations, lonely rest

stops, anyplace isolated and open to the public, or filled with loiterers.

☑ Instead of using a bus or train station's public restroom, see if the **STATION'S LUNCHEONETTE** has its own facilities. It's worth the cost of a cup of coffee.

☑ **MEN:** Choose stalls rather than urinals for more protection from trouble. Lock the door if possible. If anyone seems overly interested in you — for whatever reason — leave immediately for a well-lit, populated area.

☑ **WOMEN:** If you are concerned and no one is going into the restroom with you, ask a guard or companion to stand outside the door and wait for you. Choose a stall with one side against a wall. Don't hang your purse on the hook on the stall door — a thief can grab it and run, and you can't give chase. Hold your purse between your feet or on your lap.

☑ **CHILDREN:** Always escort your child to the restroom — never assume it's safe. Mothers can take sons five or younger into the Ladies' Room if they watch that the children don't peek under the stalls. If a boy objects to going into the Ladies' Room, enlist a trusted male to accompany him into the proper facility. Fathers shouldn't take daughters into the Men's Room

— enlist a female security guard or permanent employee to escort your child into the Ladies' Room.

☑ Remember, the response you receive depends largely on the way the request is presented. **IN A REAL EMERGENCY,** you should feel no embarrassment about saying politely and directly, *"This is an emergency, may I please use your restroom?"*

Dealing With Panhandlers

☑ **DON'T WALK IN DREAD** of panhandlers — many of them are frail and poor and aren't going to do anything to you.

☑ **DON'T FEEL OBLIGATED** to give them money.

☑ If you want to give money to a panhandler, have coins or bills ready — **NEVER OPEN YOUR PURSE** or wallet in public.

☑ Many communities provide **ALTERNATIVE GIVING OPPORTUNITIES,** so you do not have to hand money directly to a stranger on the street.

☑ If a panhandler becomes aggressive, get away immediately. **DON'T BE DRAWN INTO** a verbal or physical confrontation.

Taxi Trips

☑ **STAY FOCUSED** when hailing a taxi — don't let your luggage or briefcase out of your sight.

☑ Some cities post **TAXI GUIDELINES** at the airport: how to identify legitimate cabs, ride costs to landmarks and hotels, and how to complain if there's a problem or accident. If guidelines are not posted, ask at the ground transportation counter or check with someone local for about how much the ride should cost.

☑ **SEEK OUT LEGITIMATE CABS** whenever possible — don't get into a taxi if you can't see a medallion or the operator's photo ID. Unlicensed "gypsy" cabs operate illegally in many cities — and they may not have sufficient insurance. Be suspicious if anyone approaches you at the airport saying no taxis or shuttle buses are available, and offers to take you himself.

☑ **ASK A LOCAL** to recommend a reliable cab company. Carry the phone number with you.

☑ **KNOW THE APPROXIMATE DISTANCE** to your destination. If you suspect the driver is padding the meter by taking long routes or wrong turns, copy down his name and then speak up.

☑ When you get in, note when the driver **RESETS THE METER.** You're charged for time as well as mileage. In cities where cabs charge fees by the zone, make sure you and the driver agree on the fare before you shut the cab door.

☑ If you have only **A COUPLE OF BAGS**, put them into the backseat with you instead of into the trunk. This will allow you to make a quick exit if you feel unsafe.

☑ Think twice about **SHARING A CAB** with a stranger. If your gut reaction is negative, say no.

☑ **JOT DOWN THE NAME** of the driver and the number of the cab. At worst, you can toss it away later. At best, you'll have a way to track dishonesty or retrieve anything you leave behind.

☑ If **ERRATIC DRIVING** makes you feel unsafe, don't hesitate to tell the driver to slow down and drive carefully. It's your life he's compromising.

☑ **WEAR YOUR SEATBELT** — if you can find it.

☑ Your taxi driver can be a **FOUNTAIN OF INFORMATION** about the city. Ask about unsafe neighborhoods and any problem areas near your hotel — as well as sights to see, special attractions and local restaurants.

☑ Pay the driver **INSIDE THE CAB**. Don't flash money outside the door.

☑ At your destination, **ASK THE DRIVER TO WAIT** until you are safely inside. If he can accompany you to the door, tip him well for this extra service.

☑ If you suspect you're **BEING OVERCHARGED**, jot down the complaint number displayed in the taxi. If you realize the rip-off after you've left the cab, call the company and ask for a supervisor.

City Mobility Smarts

☑ **YOU MAY BE BETTER OFF** taking a taxi than trying to navigate your car through crowded, unfamiliar streets.

☑ Listen to the **NEWS AND TRAFFIC REPORTS** on the radio — in addition to traffic snarls, listen for situations that could become dangerous in areas of an unfamiliar city.

☑ **DON'T HANG YOUR ARM OUT THE WINDOW.** It's not only dangerous, it advertises your expensive rings and wristwatch.

☑ When asking directions or making dinner reservations, also **ASK WHERE TO PARK.**

Parking Lot Smarts

☑ **THE IDEAL PARKING LOT** is brightly lit, with a limited number of exits and entrances and uniformed security guards.

☑ Just because you don't see trouble doesn't mean it isn't there. **BE ON GUARD** when entering or returning to a parking lot, especially an empty one.

☑ **PARK AS CLOSE AS YOU CAN** to the main elevator, escalator or stairway, which will be near the marked handicapped spaces. Try to park on the main level so you won't have to take any stairs or elevators.

☑ **DON'T PARK IN A SPACE** that gives your hotel room number. And don't let the valet tag your car that way.

☑ Watch out for **DRIVERS IGNORING DIRECTIONAL ARROWS** and darting to claim parking spaces.

☑ **IF THE LOT IS FULL,** look for other well-lit areas to park your car, as close as possible to your hotel or restaurant entrance.

☑ You will be more successful finding **A SPOT IN A CROWDED LOT** if you turn off the radio, crack open the window and listen for engines starting up.

☑ Unless you must display it, **TAKE YOUR PARKING STUB** — leaving it makes it easier for a thief to take your car without raising suspicion. You'll be glad you have it with you if parking validation is available.

☑ Remember **WHERE YOU'RE PARKED** — or jot it down on the back of your parking stub.

☑ If you return to your car just to **DROP OFF PACKAGES,** move the car to a different section of the lot. Put the items in the trunk *before* you move the car.

☑ **MAKE SURE THE GUY** taking your car is really the parking valet. Check for another matching uniform if possible. If you have any suspicions, smile, shake your head, and drive back out again.

☑ When a valet parks your car, **GIVE ONLY THE IGNITION KEY** — keep the key for the trunk. If your car has an interior trunk latch, don't leave anything in the trunk.

☑ **NEVER LEAVE YOUR CAR** running and unattended. Don't walk away until the valet has secured your car.

☑ When **RETURNING TO YOUR CAR** in a self-park lot, don't zigzag between parked cars. Walk down the main rows and keep your eyes open. CHECK THE BACK SEAT of your car to be sure no one is hiding there. If anything seems different, go and get help.

City Parking Smarts

☑ Try not to park **NEXT TO POTENTIAL HIDING PLACES,** like shrubbery, Dumpsters or vans. Avoid side streets and alleys. Look around from inside the car before getting out.

☑ **IF YOU'LL RETURN AFTER DARK,** park where you will be safer: under a street light, near a cashier's booth or surveillance camera or close to store or hotel entrances. Be sure those stores won't be closed when you return. Well-lit, attended parking areas are worth a few extra dollars.

☑ Turn your steering wheel **SHARPLY TOWARD THE CURB** to make it tougher for a thief to tow your car.

☑ **MAKE THE CAR LOOK EMPTY.** Don't leave anything in plain view — even leather day planners get stolen. Thieves don't know that boxes or bags are empty until they've broken into your car. Ask yourself, *"Is there anything in this car that I could bear never to see again?"* If yes, don't leave it in the car — take it with you.

☑ **DON'T TRY TO HIDE PACKAGES,** stereos or clothing under towels or newspapers.

☑ Always empty the car every night. **IF YOU MUST**

LEAVE THINGS IN THE TRUNK, load them at a stop BEFORE you arrive, so no one can see you stowing valuables. Make the trunk less accessible by backing the car as close as possible to a wall.

☑ Don't advertise you're from out of town. **HIDE TELLTALE MAPS,** travel brochures and luggage.

☑ Double check your inside **DOME LIGHT.** Leaving it on is one of the leading causes of dead batteries.

☑ If your state doesn't require a front license plate on your vehicle, back into parking spaces — thieves won't see your **OUT-OF-STATE PLATE.**

☑ Pay particular attention to parking restrictions in **HISTORIC DISTRICTS AND TOURIST ATTRACTIONS.** They may be more vigorously enforced.

☑ The underside of your car gets very hot: **DON'T PARK OVER PAPERS,** leaves, dry grass or anything that can burn.

☑ About **20 PACES FROM THE CAR,** glance back to make sure your car is secure in its surroundings, and you haven't left any lights on.

☑ If your **CAR IS MISSING WHEN YOU RETURN,** there are three possibilities. You've mistaken the location, it's been stolen, or it's been towed. Look for a posted towing phone number. If you see broken glass on the street where you are certain your car was, call the police immediately.

Returning To Your Car

☑ Don't stand at your car fumbling for your keys. **HAVE YOUR CAR KEY IN YOUR HAND,** especially at night.

☑ If you're alone at a shopping mall, **ASK MALL SECU-RITY TO ESCORT YOU** to your car.

☑ If you see or **SENSE SOMEONE HANGING AROUND YOUR CAR,** KEEP WALKING. Make sure no one is crouched beside the passenger door or under your car. From a distance, bend over slightly and look under your vehicle for anyone hiding.

☑ **DON'T RELY ON EARLIER OBSERVATIONS** — things may have changed since you parked your car. People may have left, businesses may have closed, new people may now be loitering. Check again on your return.

☑ If your **ELECTRONIC DOOR LOCKS** all automatically open at the same time, double check for anyone lurking near the far side of your car.

☑ **GLANCE AT THE BACK SEAT** before getting in —

make sure no one's hiding there. In a two-door vehicle, leave your seatbacks pushed forward so you can easily notice anything different on your return.

☑ If the car won't start, or you have a flat tire, **THE PROBLEM COULD BE DELIBERATE.** Scan the street for anything suspicious; get out of the car, lock the door and seek assistance at the nearest well-lit, populated place. Don't accept a stranger's offer of help — he may have disabled your car.

☑ **IF YOUR CAR HAS BEEN BROKEN INTO,** don't touch anything that could smudge fingerprints or disturb evidence. Call police.

☑ Do everything possible NOT to get into a car with an attacker. Statistically, your chances are better if you **STAY OUT OF THE CAR.**

Subway Smarts

☑ When purchasing tokens or farecards, **DON'T FLASH WADS OF CASH.** Have small bills ready.

☑ Buy your **ROUND-TRIP FARE IN ADVANCE,** whether it's by token or farecard. If you'll be using the subway again, purchase several roundtrips.

☑ **TURN THE STONE** of your rings around toward the

palm of your hand. Tuck necklaces inside your shirt.

☑ Don't stand on **EMPTY OR DIMLY LIT PLATFORMS** during off-hours. Stand near transit police, in specially designated off-hours waiting areas or near manned token booths — outside the turnstile if possible.

☑ **DON'T ENTER AN EMPTY CAR**. Middle cars on subway trains are usually more populated.

☑ **PICKPOCKETS** often work the crowd on the platform or inside the train. Secure your wallet and valuables. See page 131.

☑ Check the local yellow pages — they often include **SUBWAY MAPS**. If you have time, call the transit system and ask for a map.

☑ Ask the concierge or call information for any **FREE ASSISTANCE NUMBERS** the local transit system provides. Carry that number with you.

☑ Ask at the kiosk **WHICH PLATFORM TO STAND** on for your destination. At the platform, double check with a guard that you are in the right place.

☑ Make sure you are not boarding an **EXPRESS TRAIN** unless you mean to — express trains skip many stops.

☑ Don't discuss your personal business or travel plans

in public, or **WITHIN EARSHOT OF STRANGERS.**

☑ **STAY ALERT** on the subway. Don't fall asleep, don't get too absorbed in reading, don't listen to your portable stereo.

☑ Don't put your briefcase or **PURSE ON THE SEAT NEXT TO YOU.** Keep it on your lap or secure between your legs.

☑ Get up and **CHANGE YOUR SEAT** the instant you feel uncomfortable or intimidated. Do not wait.

☑ **IF THE CAR YOU'RE ON BECOMES EMPTY** before you reach your station, get up and move to a more populated car.

☑ **DON'T SIT NEXT TO A DOOR.** Thieves can grab your valuables and run as the doors close.

City Bus Smarts

☑ **BE ALERT** at crowded bus stops where pickpockets like to work. Don't stand in the middle of a crowd.

☑ Have **CORRECT CHANGE** or small bills ready in hand.

☑ Sit in **CLEAR VIEW OF THE DRIVER** and away from the rear exit. Purse snatchers can grab your belongings on their way out the door.

☑ **WATCH** who gets on and off. Be especially alert if anyone sits right next to you when there are many other seats available.

☑ Avoid **CONFRONTATIONAL STARES** with strangers. If you feel someone's staring at you, look up quickly to ascertain if there is any danger — then drop your eyes.

☑ If any other passengers make you feel uneasy or unsafe, seriously weigh the possibility of **GETTING OFF THE BUS** at a well-lit, populated stop. Paying an additional fare to complete the ride is preferable to being at risk.

☑ If you get off a bus in an **AREA THAT MAKES YOU UNEASY**, see if there is an open store or gas station you can go to. If not, stay out in the open at the bus stop and try to catch another bus — or a taxi.

If You Are Confronted

☑ Each circumstance is different — only you can assess your best options. It's best to err on the side of safety. Possessions can be replaced, but your life is priceless. Right now while you have time, read the next three pages and go over in your mind what you can do if confronted. Have your **ACTION PLAN LAID OUT.**

☑ If someone in a car threatens you while you are walking or jogging, turn quickly and **RUN IN THE OPPOSITE DIRECTION** from the way the car is going. If you can safely cross the street behind the car and run in the opposite direction, that's even better.

☑ If you feel you are in danger, **SCREAM FORCEFULLY,** "NO!" "GET AWAY!" or "CALL POLICE!" If you've got a loud whistle or pocket shriek alarm, use it. If others are around, yell to them to "CALL 911!" The more attention you attract, the better your chances for witnesses to get a good description of your assailant.

☑ If you are **DIRECTLY CONFRONTED** by a robber — cooperate as best you can. Hand over your money, valuables and anything you are asked for. Don't risk physical injury. Try to stay calm. Don't resist. Don't argue. Don't move suddenly. Don't show hostility. Don't give steady eye contact. Don't assume there is no weapon just because you don't see one. Don't anger your assailant or any accomplices — they may be young, nervous, high or in need of a fix.

☑ **DON'T MOUTH-OFF** or act macho; don't talk and don't joke. Wisecracking or verbal threats only work in movies — nowadays they greatly increase your chance of injury. Keep your mouth shut. If you are asked anything, listen carefully, and reply briefly in a neutral or calming voice. Tell your assailant that you're reaching for your wallet — avoid sudden motions.

☑ After you've handed over your money and valuables, you are at your most vulnerable. **WAIT CALMLY** for him to leave. If he tells you to lie down on the ground, do it. Don't speak unless asked, and do not give chase.

☑ **TRY TO AVOID BEING MOVED** into an alley, doorway or other hidden place.

☑ In all cases, do whatever you can not to be forced into a car with your assailant. Run, scream, fight, escape. Your odds are infinitely better if you **DON'T GET INTO THE CAR.**

☑ If you take action, be prepared to **FOLLOW ALL THE WAY THROUGH** with it. If you try to escape, be certain you can succeed. If you fight to defend yourself, don't stop until you are sure your attacker is disabled, or runs away. Consider taking a self-defense course, where you'll learn effective techniques to handle an attacker.

☑ **TRY TO REMEMBER DETAILS** about your assailant.

Particularly look for height, weight, approximate age, scars, birthmarks, tattoos and any other distinguishing characteristics. Details of clothing are less helpful, since they are most easily changed. Try to get a license plate number.

☑ **REPORT ANY ROBBERY** or mugging to police, even if you were not hurt or nothing much was taken. Your report can help take a criminal off the streets. Be sure to get a copy of the police report for insurance and tax purposes.

☑ **ASSESS WHAT WAS TAKEN.** You may need to notify your bank, credit cards, car rental agency and hotel right away. (Use your photocopied information — see page 13). You may need to change house and car locks if your keys were stolen, and alert friends and relatives if your address book was taken.

☑ **CHECK NEARBY ALLEYS**, trash cans, Dumpsters and restrooms to see if the thief tossed away your wallet or purse after removing the cash and credit cards.

Hotel & Motel Smarts

The Call-Ahead Lodging Security Checklist

☐ Is there only one entrance? Does it lead directly to the front desk?

☐ Is the front desk staffed 24-hours a day?

☐ Are there security officers around-the-clock?

☐ Do you receive a programmable key card instead of a metal key?

☐ Does your room open to a secure corridor or directly to the outside?

☐ Does the door have a peephole or side panel to give you a full view of people outside your door? Is the corridor lighting bright enough to see them?

☐ Does the door have a deadbolt lock and security chain or bar?

☐ Does locking the deadbolt from the inside prevent entry by all but emergency master keys?

☐ Are the room doors self-closing? Do they lock automatically?

☐ Does the room have a smoke detector and fire sprinkler?

☐ Will your room have its own safe?

☐ Are the parking lots well-lit, monitored and accessible directly from the hotel?

Reservation Savvy

☑ Always **WRITE DOWN THE NAME** of the employee you spoke with, plus any reservation number, in case of a lost reservation or other snafu.

☑ Be sure the guidebook you're using to select accommodations **RATES HOTELS AND MOTELS IMPARTIALLY,** separate from corporate tie-ins and paid advertorials.

☑ Some of the better guidebooks list accommodations with **IN-ROOM SMOKE DETECTORS** and sprinkler systems. If your guidebook doesn't, ask.

☑ Ask whether the hotel has **METAL KEYS OR CARD KEYS** — electronic "keyless" locks are safer because they can be recoded for each guest. Most also create an electronic log of who goes in and out of your room, as a strong deterrent to internal theft.

☑ For fire safety reasons, request a room on the **THIRD FLOOR OR BELOW** if there is no sprinkler system; but for safety from burglary, stay above the ground floor.

☑ If a ground floor room is unavoidable, ask for one that opens onto an **INTERIOR HALLWAY WITH LIMITED ACCESS** to outsiders.

☑ If your room will be accessible from walkways and common balconies, ask if it has **ADDITIONAL SECURITY LOCKS ON WINDOWS** and sliding doors.

☑ If you **CALL THE LOCAL POLICE**, they probably won't tell you about specific crimes, but you can request statistics on crimes committed in the surrounding area.

☑ If you'll arrive after the lodging's official check-in time, **GUARANTEE YOUR ROOM** with your credit card.

☑ Ask if the facility offers a **FREE AIRPORT SHUTTLE** or limo. Find out where you need to meet it.

☑ Get the **DIRECTIONS AND DISTANCE** from the airport or highway. Ask where to park.

☑ For extra security, **BUY A PORTABLE DOOR LOCK**, available from travel supply stores and catalogs. But remember these locks prevent entry from the outside so well, that someone would have to break the door down if you needed help.

☑ Dress casually for your arrival, and leave the jewelry at home. **DON'T APPEAL TO POTENTIAL THIEVES.**

☑ Remember, **PRICE IS NOT AN INDICATION OF SECURITY.** Reject any hotel that doesn't meet your standards or expectations.

Arriving At The Hotel

☑ Keep your **BAGS AT YOUR FEET** at all times — especially out on the sidewalk while trying to locate the bell staff.

☑ **SURVEY THE LOBBY AS YOU ENTER:** Is it clean, orderly and well-lit? Is the bell staff offering to help with your luggage? Are keys lying around on the front desk? Is anyone unsavory loitering? If anything gives you a bad reaction (like a cashier enclosed in bulletproof glass), don't be afraid to go elsewhere.

☑ If you guaranteed your reservation with a credit card — but there are no rooms when you arrive — **THE HOTEL SHOULD "WALK" YOU** to alternate comparable accommodations. Generally, you will be offered a free night at the alternate hotel, plus transportation there and a phone call to advise your family of the change.

☑ Tell them you want a **ROOM NEAR AN ELEVATOR,** but not right next to it. Avoid rooms down long deserted hallways, next to stairwells or adjacent to balcony walkways.

☑ If the hotel has **OUTDOOR PARKING**, request a room that overlooks your parked car. But don't park in a space that displays your room number. And don't let them place a sticker on your car indicating your room number.

☑ You can ask to **SEE THE ROOM BEFORE YOU TAKE IT.** Make sure it meets your standards for security, and has all the amenities you've requested. If not, ask for a different room.

☑ Ask **WHAT THE FIRE ALARM SOUNDS LIKE.** Many people don't leave when they hear the alarm, because they don't recognize its purpose.

☑ Don't ask about the **HOTEL SAFE** in a loud voice or say what you plan to put in it. Once you're in the room, prepare the things you want to put into the safe. Then call the front desk.

☑ If the hotel uses metal keys, yours **SHOULD NOT SHOW YOUR ROOM NUMBER,** hotel name or any identification. Beware of hotels with simplistic key markings — one digit added to the room number makes it easy for burglars to use the key.

☑ If you can't accompany the bell staff and your luggage to your room, at least **GET THE NAME OF THE BELL STAFF** person and find out how soon the luggage will be delivered.

The 60-Second Security Scan

☑ **AFTER THE BELL STAFF UNLOAD YOUR LUGGAGE,** make sure they check that your room is secure: Are all doors to connecting rooms locked? Even on upper floors, do all windows and sliding doors lock — yet open easily from the inside in case of fire? Does the phone work? Does it list the number for security? Make sure they check behind the shower curtain and drapes, under the bed and inside the closet. *Tip the bellstaff only after you are sure the room is safe and adequate.*

☑ **IF NO BELL STAFF ACCOMPANY YOU,** check the hallway to be sure no one is loitering; then put your heaviest bag against the room door to prop it open. Quickly survey the room for the major safety points listed above. When the room passes, pull in your bag and lock the door.

☑ Make sure **THE DOOR TO YOUR ROOM LOCKS SECURELY,** isn't misaligned and isn't obstructed by faulty locks or new high-pile carpeting. Check your key in the outside lock; if you are dissatisfied, call the front desk immediately.

☑ **MAKE A MENTAL MAP OF THE HALLWAY:** scan for fire exits in both directions. Count the doorways to each emergency exit so you could feel your way out in the dark if you had to. Find the fire extinguishers and the fire alarm.

☑ Are **EMERGENCY ESCAPE INSTRUCTIONS** displayed in your room? If they are not clear, call the front desk to answer any questions. If the instructions include a floorplan, see where your room is in relation to the exits on the map.

☑ Is the 'on' light lit on the **SMOKE DETECTOR?**

During Your Stay

☑ Before anything else, use the **HOTEL SAFE** to store your airline tickets, passport, electronic equipment, credit cards and cash. Seal cash and credit cards in an envelope and sign it — this makes any tampering evident immediately. Get a receipt.

☑ The hotel is not responsible for loss unless your valuables are in their safe. But **CHECK THEIR LIABILITY LIMIT** — some are covered for only a few hundred dollars' loss!

☑ When you're settled in, **CALL YOUR AIRLINE AND GIVE THEM YOUR HOTEL PHONE NUMBER** so they can reach you if there's a schedule change or cancellation.

☑ **LOCK YOUR LUGGAGE** — even if it's empty — so nobody can use your own bags to cart off your possessions.

☑ **DON'T LEAVE YOUR CREDIT CARD RECEIPTS OUT** — they give thieves all the information needed to use your account, plus your signature to be forged.

☑ **DON'T LEAVE YOUR CAR KEYS IN THE ROOM.** Stow them in the in-room safe or take them with you — even if you're just going to the pool or lounge.

☑ Don't leave fountain pens, calculators, costume jewelry or day planners in view — put them inside the drawers, on top of your clothes. (Putting them under clothes doesn't let you take a **QUICK VISUAL INVENTORY** to see if things are missing.)

☑ Using a portable drawer lock on the desk or bureau tells a burglar exactly where to look for your valuables. **USE THE SAFE.**

☑ Hang your **EXPENSIVE ARTICLES OF CLOTHING** in the closet underneath your less-costly clothes.

☑ **USE THE YELLOW PAGES** as a safety reference. The directory includes numbers for police, fire, poison control, as well as airport layout. If your room doesn't have a copy, ask for one.

☑ **WHEN YOU LEAVE THE ROOM**, make it look like someone is still there — leave on a light, the TV and the fan. Open the closet and bathroom doors completely to give you full view of the room when you return. Lock the windows and close the curtains.

☑ **DON'T USE THE "MAID" DOORHANGER** — it telegraphs you're not there, and the maid will check your room anyway. If your room has already been cleaned, hang the "Do Not Disturb" sign on the door before you go out.

During Your Stay

☑ Every time you come or go, **DOUBLE-CHECK TO MAKE SURE THE DOOR IS LOCKED**. Don't assume that the door will close automatically and latch by itself every time.

☑ Be especially **CAREFUL WITH YOUR ROOM KEY** or card key — guard it at poolside, in the lounge or in the restaurant.

☑ **DON'T COMPROMISE YOUR ROOM NUMBER**. If you sign for food or drinks to be billed to your room, turn the check face down or hand it directly to the waiter. Leaving the check face up shows your room number to everyone.

☑ Take a moment to mark the street map you're carrying with the **LOCATION OF YOUR HOTEL.**

☑ Make sure you have the **PHONE NUMBER OF THE HOTEL** with you, but don't write it on the card key. Keep one of their business cards with you in your wallet.

☑ **WOMEN:** See page 183 for more hotel safety tips.

☑ When you return to the hotel **LATE IN THE EVENING,** use the main entrance. Have your key in-hand before you get to your room. If you feel uneasy, ask a hotel employee to escort you.

☑ If you feel you're being followed to your room, **DON'T GO IN.** Walk to the front desk and tell hotel management.

☑ If you're uncomfortable **PARKING YOUR CAR AT NIGHT,** drive to the front entrance and ask a hotel employee to accompany you while you park.

☑ If you observe any suspicious activity, **DON'T BE SHY** about reporting it immediately to hotel security or the front desk.

☑ **IF YOU LIKE TO JOG,** ask the front desk to recommend a safe route.

In-Room Safety

☑ **NEVER INVITE STRANGERS UP TO YOUR ROOM.**

☑ **LOCK ALL DOORS COMPLETELY** whenever you're in the room, using all the locks and security devices provided. When you're in the shower, lock the windows and balcony door, too.

☑ Don't leave the **BALCONY DOOR** open while you sleep — yours can be accessed from other balconies. Use the air conditioner or fan for ventilation.

☑ Get in the habit of keeping your **ROOM KEY IN THE SAME PLACE** at every hotel (on the nightstand, top of the TV, etc.). This will save you looking for it, and facilitates a quick exit in an emergency. It also helps prevent being locked out when the emergency's over.

☑ Keep a **FLASHLIGHT ON YOUR NIGHTSTAND.** If you forget one, most drugstores stock them for less than five dollars. Don't become one of the many who stub or break toes trying to find the bathroom in a dark hotel room or get out in an emergency. Don't leave suitcases or chairs between your bed and the door.

☑ **DON'T OPEN THE DOOR** to anyone who identifies himself as "from the hotel" or "checking the smoke detector." First, call the front desk to confirm his identity and purpose.

☑ If you order **FOOD FROM A LOCAL TAKEOUT**, meet the delivery person in the lobby. Ask the front desk to call you when your food arrives. Don't let anyone come up to your room.

☑ Stay alert going to the ice or vending machine. Bring your key — **DON'T PROP THE DOOR OPEN**, even if you're only gone for a minute.

☑ If the hotel gives you two room keys **DON'T LEAVE THE EXTRA KEY** lying around in the room. Someone could pocket it and use it later.

☑ **IF YOU MAKE COFFEE** with an in-room coffeemaker or your own immersion heater, TURN IT OFF when you're finished.

☑ If you **THINK YOU HEAR SOMEONE** trying to get into your room during the night, shout *"Bruno, I think I hear a burglar"* — especially if there is no Bruno.

☑ Consider a **PORTABLE DOOR ALARM,** available through catalogs and travel specialty stores. If you don't have one and you feel nervous, you can make one — take the flat, shallow drawer out of the desk and hook the edge over the top of the door molding. Be careful in the morning — don't get conked on the head.

☑ Don't get **SCALDED BY AN UNFAMILIAR SHOWER.**
First run only the hot water, until it reaches maximum
heat — then adjust the cold water until the mix gets to
your desired comfort level. And be careful if the shower
floor isn't an anti-slip surface.

Before You Check Out

☑ Places to check before checking out:

☐ Shower stall   ☐ Balcony
☐ Under the bed   ☐ Drawers
☐ The in-room safe   ☐ Closet
☐ The hotel safe   ☐ Medicine cabinet

Checking Out

☑ Keep your **BAGS BY YOUR FEET** at all times when
you're waiting for transportation. Watch to see that
they're placed in the right cab or shuttle bus.

☑ If there's a lot of time between check-out and your
flight, ask if the hotel can **STORE YOUR LUGGAGE** *in a
secure location* until you come back — not on a luggage cart in the lobby.

Escaping A Hotel Fire

➔ **HAVE AN ESCAPE PLAN READY** for you and your family. You'll reduce panic and dramatically increase your chances of survival. Remember: *it's not the fire, it's the smoke.* Try to stay in hotels and motels with sprinkler systems.

➔ **IF A FIRE BREAKS OUT IN YOUR ROOM:**

❶ Grab your key and exit the room.

❷ Close the door tightly behind you.

❸ Sound the fire alarm and alert hotel employees.

❹ Pound on neighboring doors to alert other guests.

❺ Do not get on the elevator.

❻ Walk down the stairs to a safe place.

➔ **IF YOU HEAR THE FIRE ALARM FROM YOUR ROOM, IF YOU SMELL SMOKE, OR IF YOU HEAR A COMMOTION OUTSIDE YOUR ROOM:**

❶ DON'T roll over and go back to sleep.

❷ Before dashing into the hallway, FEEL THE DOOR FOR HEAT. Never open a hot door — you risk letting smoke and fire into your room.

→ IF THE DOOR IS **NOT HOT:**

❶ Call the front desk. Ask for the location of the fire.

❷ Peek out into the hallway to check for smoke.

❸ *If there is NO smoke*, grab your key, close your door and walk down the stairs to a safe place. Don't stop for your belongings. And NEVER take the elevator — even if you suspect it's a false alarm.

❹ *If there is the SMELL of smoke*, walk down the stairs to a safe place. Make sure you bring your key in case exits are blocked or all stairwells are filled with smoke and you must return to your room. Knock on neighboring doors to warn others.

❺ *If the smoke is THICK*, wrap a wet towel over your mouth and nose and crawl out — the air will be fresher at floor level. Close the door behind you to keep the fire from spreading into your room. Stay against the wall on the side of the exit. If you have a child with you, put him on your back.

❻ *If the smoke is TOO THICK*, or you are unable to go down a stairwell, you may be able to go up to the roof. If there is an openable roof door, let others know you're on the roof, stay out of the path of smoke and wait for help.

➔ IF THE DOOR IS HOT, OR IF THE HALLWAY IS FILLED WITH SMOKE, OF IF EXITS ARE BLOCKED:

❶ Stay in your room and be prepared to fight the fire. You can survive.

❷ Make sure the door is tightly shut.

❸ Call the front desk or 911 for help. Give your room number.

❹ If there is no smoke outdoors, open the windows or sliding door to vent the room — but don't break the glass. If you're on the first or second floor, you may be able to drop safely to the ground. If you're on a higher floor, you risk severe injury if you jump.

❺ Fill the bathtub with water and dunk towels and sheets — then stuff them under doors and in air vents to seal out smoke. Turn off the air conditioner and set to "recirculate" to block smoke coming through vent.

❻ Turn on the bathroom fan for added venting — unless it increases smoke or draws it from other places. Then turn off the fan and use a wet towel to seal it.

❼ Scoop water out of the bathtub with a wastebasket or ice bucket. Toss water on hot walls and doors. Keep the doors, walls and carpet wet.

❽ If your window opens, hang a sheet to tell rescuers where to find you. Don't climb down the sheet. Listen to firefighters for instructions. Remove curtains or drapes, and get them away from the windows.

➔ IF SMOKE HAS ENTERED YOUR ROOM:

❾ Stand at an open window to breathe fresh air. Place a wet towel or sheet over your mouth and nose. If the window does not open — and you are low enough to the ground to escape — you may have to break the glass with a chair. Use a blanket to help shield yourself from any remaining jagged glass. It is not recommended that you break the glass if you're on an upper story — it can let more smoke into the room and injure firefighters below with falling shards of glass.

❿ As a last resort, if it becomes impossible to remain in the room any longer, you may be forced to go for the best exit. Keep a wet towel over your mouth and nose and crawl out.

Every-body's Smarts

USA

Hotel Smarts For Women

See also Hotel Smarts — page 163.

☑ Register using **ONLY YOUR LAST NAME** and first initial, without Mrs. or Ms.

☑ If any hotel help **ANNOUNCES YOUR ROOM NUMBER** loud enough for others to hear it, say you want a different room.

☑ **KEEP YOUR ROOM NUMBER TO YOURSELF.** Meet new acquaintances in busy public places like restaurants and lobbies.

☑ When choosing lodging, check whether incoming calls go through a hotel operator. For safety's sake, it's better if callers must **ASK FOR GUESTS BY NAME** — not by room number.

☑ Don't use gyms, pools or saunas if they **AREN'T IN PLAIN VIEW,** or no attendant is present.

☑ **NEVER TAKE THE STAIRS** to your room. You are isolated in a stairwell.

☑ If you **FEEL YOU'RE BEING FOLLOWED,** don't go to your room — go to the front desk. In an emergency, bang on a room door and yell, *"Bruno, let's go...we're late!"*

City Smarts For Women

See also City Smarts — page 127.

☑ **MEMORIZE A FEW FOREIGN PHRASES.** If anyone accosts you or asks for money, you can say, *"Garbage in season is riper at home"* in Phoenician. Keep walking.

☑ **YOUR CHILD CAN BE THE DISTRACTION** that thieves need to grab your valuables. Carry your belongings in ways that let you still tend to your child.

☑ Married or not, consider **WEARING A WEDDING RING.** It may not repel hardcore wolves, but it sends a message that you won't welcome being bothered.

☑ When walking outside, wear gloves or keep the **STONES OF ANY RINGS** inward toward your palm.

☑ Alcohol slows you down and increases your vulnerability. **PARTY WISELY** in unfamiliar surroundings.

☑ If a man offers unwanted attention, state that you are not interested. **BE FIRM, CLEAR AND LOUD.**

☑ If you're dressed for a night on the town, **WEAR AN OVERCOAT** if you feel you could attract the wrong kind of attention on the way.

☑ If you're being verbally abused, **DON'T RESPOND.** Walk quickly toward a populated, well-lit area.

Purse Smarts

☑ In public, **KEEP YOUR PURSE ON YOU** at all times.

☑ Carry your purse firmly **UNDER YOUR ARM, FLAP-SIDE TOWARD YOU.** Don't dangle the straps over your shoulder, and don't let the purse slip behind your back.

☑ Wearing your **SHOULDER BAG STRAP ACROSS YOUR CHEST** makes you unable to let go if your purse is grabbed. It's secure and sends a strong signal to a purse snatcher, but you risk being dragged along, and it's still equally easy to cut off. It's your personal decision how you wish to show control over your purse.

☑ **WEAR YOUR PURSE UNDER YOUR COAT.** Or hide your purse inside a shopping bag and hold both sets of handles. On planes, leave room in your carry-on bag to pack your purse.

☑ Don't carry a purse if you don't really need one. **WEAR A JACKET WITH POCKETS** and divide your things to carry on you.

☑ **KEEP BOTH HANDS AS FREE AS POSSIBLE.** Loading yourself down with suitcases makes you vulnerable.

☑ **CHOOSE A PURSE WITH A FLAP,** a tight clasp and a zippered inner compartment big enough for your wallet. Always close and zip or fasten your purse.

☑ **ON THE STREET,** watch for purse snatchers who work from bicycles, motorcycles and from passing cars.

☑ **IN RESTAURANTS AND THEATERS,** never sling your purse over the back of a chair or leave it on the empty seat next to you. Keep it wedged between your feet.

☑ **IN PUBLIC RESTROOMS,** don't hang your purse on the hook inside the stall door. A thief can lift it from the other side, and you're in no position to give chase.

☑ Carry **IDENTIFICATION IN YOUR PURSE** separate from your wallet, listing your last name and work number. If your purse is stolen and the wallet is removed, your purse might still be returned to you.

☑ **DON'T CARRY ANYTHING IRREPLACEABLE** — like the only photo of your grandmother — in your purse.

☑ Mentally rehearse: **IF YOUR PURSE WERE GRABBED,** you'll let go and make noise. Try to get a description of the thief, but don't give chase. Nothing in your purse is worth your life — pack the contents that way, and be sure any male companion knows you value his safety over your lipstick. Until police arrive, try to recall as much as you can about your assailant.

Airplane Smarts For Women

☑ You can **ASK AT CHECK-IN** to be seated next to another female passenger.

☑ If you **DON'T WANT TO SPEAK TO YOUR SEATMATE**, wear headphones. You don't need a tape player — tuck the wire into your pocket.

☑ **PREGNANT WOMEN** should consult a doctor. Carry proof of the pregnancy's length, since some airlines won't allow flights after the 36th week without a doctor's permission. Check with your doctor about flights during the first and last trimesters. Walk the cabin every half hour, drink plenty of fluids, fasten the seatbelt low around the pelvis, and book an aisle seat for easy lavatory access.

City Smarts For Men

☑ Put a wide **RUBBER BAND AROUND YOUR WALLET** — that prevents it from being slipped out of your pocket easily.

☑ Keep your **WALLET IN YOUR FRONT PANTS POCKET** or in an inside jacket pocket — never in your back pocket!

☑ **AN ARMED FEMALE** is just as dangerous as an armed male. This is no time to indulge your macho impulses. Hand over your money.

Solo City Smarts

☑ **LEAVE YOUR ITINERARY** and contact number with someone who can take action if anything goes wrong.

☑ Book your lodging at **HOTELS WITH DINING FACILITIES** and room service. That way, you won't have to go exploring to find a meal.

☑ Consider staying at a **BED & BREAKFAST,** where you can also meet new and interesting people.

City Business Smarts

☑ At conventions and seminars, **REMOVE YOUR NAME BADGE** before leaving the facility.

☑ **STOW YOUR CONVENTION LITERATURE** — or carry it in a plain shopping bag. Displaying brightly-colored convention freebies identifies you as an out-of-towner.

☑ Don't put your purse or valuables in **CONVENTION GIVEAWAY BAGS.** Yours can easily be confused with the thousands of similar bags.

☑ Set up a **BUDDY SYSTEM** with a colleague and check back with each other at agreed-upon times.

☑ Instruct the people at your office and your home — **DON'T REVEAL YOUR TRAVEL PLANS.**

☑ Before entering meeting rooms, note the location of the **FIRE EXITS.**

☑ **DON'T ACCEPT RIDES** from people you don't know — even if they say they are attending your meeting.

☑ **ALWAYS CARRY A MINI-FLASHLIGHT** in your brief-case — with fresh batteries.

☑ **TIGHTEN ANY LOOSE HANDLES** or weak latches on your briefcase, laptop or notebook computer.

☑ Call your hotel in advance to be sure their **IN-ROOM SAFE IS BIG ENOUGH** to hold your computer.

☑ **LABELING THE CASE ISN'T ENOUGH.** Tape your business card or identification number securely onto the bottom of your laptop, power adapter, modem, mouse, etc. Write "Please call collect" on the cards.

☑ **AT AIRPORT SECURITY,** you may be asked to boot up. Make sure your batteries are fully charged, or your power adapter is handy. Have a program available to run that displays text rather than graphics.

☑ Don't carry your diskettes on you through the **AIR-PORT METAL DETECTOR.** Send them through the X-ray machine with your laptop.

☑ **CONSIDER LEAVING YOUR PRINTER HOME.** For a hard copy, modem a fax to yourself at the hotel. Choose hotels that offer in-room fax machines.

☑ Check whether your **BUSINESS INSURANCE COVERS THE LOSS** of any electronics carried with you. Data-loss policies may also be available to cover the cost of retrieving data from a damaged hard drive.

☑ **CARRY INDISPENSABLE WORK ITEMS** with you on the plane. Leaving samples, cards and order forms inside checked luggage can be costly if the luggage is lost.

City Smarts For Kids®

☑ **REPEAT YOUR WARNINGS** about talking to strangers or accepting gifts or rides. Teach your children to scream, run away and tell you immediately if anyone tries to bother or grab them.

☑ **MAKE SURE YOUR CHILDREN ALL KNOW** their full name, address, city, state and phone number with area code — plus both parents' first and last names. Make sure they know not to reveal this information to anyone except a police officer, doctor or nurse.

☑ **TEACH YOUR CHILDREN TO DIAL "911" or "O"** wherever they are — and when it's appropriate to call.

☑ Teach your children **IF THEY GET LOST** to seek help from a police officer, security guard, airline agent or lifeguard. Before going to sightseeing attractions, always agree where to rendezvous if they get lost.

☑ **HOLD HANDS AS MUCH AS POSSIBLE** when crowds get dense. Use the buddy system.

☑ **ESTABLISH A FAMILY CODE WORD.** Tell your children never to go with anyone who doesn't know the secret code word.

☑ Carry a good, current, **FULL-FACE PHOTO OF EACH CHILD** with you, and leave one with a trusted friend.

☑ Don't display the **CHILD'S FIRST NAME** on clothes, luggage or tags.

☑ **SET A GOOD EXAMPLE** for your children — always lock all doors and windows. Show them how to do it.

☑ **A TODDLER SAFETY STRAP** could save you from losing your child. Or consider an electronic beeper that sounds off when your child steps out of range.

☑ Develop a **DISTINCT WHISTLE OR SOUND PATTERN** your kids can listen for if they get lost. If you can't whistle, carry a coach's whistle — or give your kids whistles to use only if they're lost.

☑ Always **ESCORT YOUR CHILDREN** to the restroom. Never assume it's safe for them to go alone.

City Smarts For Teens

☑ In certain cities, clothing may be **MISIDENTIFIED AS GANG ATTIRE.** A backwards baseball cap, a bandanna, baggy pants or certain colors can be interpreted as a sign you belong to a rival gang. It may be better to make teen fashion statements on home turf.

☑ Expensive jackets or shoes could **MAKE YOUR TEEN A TARGET**. Leave the showy stuff at home.

☑ If your teen is flying alone and the flight is cancelled or delayed, he shouldn't leave the airport to find his own lodging. Have your teen ask the airline for assistance. **NEVER LEAVE THE AIRPORT WITH A STRANGER.**

Car Smarts For Kids

☑ **EVERY CHILD SHOULD BE RESTRAINED** in the vehicle. If a child has outgrown a safety seat, get a booster seat designed for cars — and install it correctly. Never place a child in a safety seat facing an airbag.

☑ Never leave a **CHILD ALONE IN A CAR WITH THE KEYS** in the ignition or the engine idling — even to dash into a convenience store.

☑ Never hold a **BABY IN YOUR ARMS WHILE RIDING IN A VEHICLE.** Not only is it illegal, but in an accident, the force will make the baby almost impossible to hold.

☑ **NEVER USE ONE BELT TO SECURE TWO KIDS.**

☑ **AN UNSECURED SAFETY SEAT WITH NO CHILD** in it can be a hazard to other passengers in an accident. Always secure the safety seat.

Kids' Hotel Secrets

☑ Ask if the hotel has **KID-READY ROOMS,** where ashtrays, matches and drinking glasses have been removed. Ask if locks are installed on refrigerator and microwave doors, and cover guards on all electrical outlets.

☑ **BRING A NIGHTLIGHT** for your child, in case he wakes up in the middle of the night.

☑ **DISCUSS AN ESCAPE PLAN** in case of fire or other emergencies. Tell them not to use the elevator.

Traveling With Disabilities

Before You Leave

☑ To avoid unforeseen problems, find a travel agent who **SPECIALIZES IN TRAVEL FOR THE DISABLED**. It costs no more, and it's smarter than calling everyone directly.

☑ Make your reservations **AS FAR AHEAD AS POSSIBLE** — space may be limited. Make sure the person arranging your travel understands the full degree of your disability and enters the details in your booking.

☑ **GET WRITTEN CONFIRMATIONS** in the form of a detailed itinerary. Check and double check that you will receive all promised services and amenities for each segment of your journey. Take names.

☑ Call ahead for any **BROCHURES ON ACCESSIBILITY**, but remember they may not be accurate or up-to-date.

☑ The **AMERICANS WITH DISABILITIES ACT** forbids discrimination against people with disabilities in any public facility — however, rules vary by the size of a facility, and compliance varies from place to place. For information on your rights, call (800) 514-0301 for voice, or (800) 514-0383 for TDD.

☑ The day before you leave, **CONFIRM ALL ARRANGEMENTS** with each airline, hotel, car rental agency, etc.

Flying With Wheelchairs

☑ Make sure your **WHEELCHAIR IS FULLY INSURED** — standard baggage insurance doesn't cover the full value of most wheelchairs in the event of a claim.

☑ **WHEN YOU BOOK YOUR TICKET,** request any wheelchairs you'll need in the airports. On the plane, remind the flight attendant about a half hour before landing to double check that it will be waiting at the gate.

☑ Ask if the plane's **LAVATORY IS MODIFIED** for wheelchairs. If not, use the airport restroom right before boarding, and restrict liquids before and during the flight. Ask your doctor about avoiding dehydration.

☑ Make sure the **SHUTTLE BUS** or ground transportation can accommodate a power wheelchair.

☑ When you arrive at the airport, ask them to load your wheelchair **"LAST ON, FIRST OFF"** to avoid delays.

☑ Using a **POWER WHEELCHAIR?** Check in at least two hours before departure. Remove any detachable parts from the chair and carry them with you. Carry the chair's assembly instructions with you. You can reduce your chances of having the chair disassembled by using a **NON-SPILLABLE BATTERY** clearly marked 'Gel Cell.'

Otherwise, the battery must be removed and packed in a separate, leakproof container.

☑ Ask for a seat in the BULKHEAD (the first seats in any section of the plane) for extra floor space.

☑ CONNECTING FLIGHT? Schedule adequate time between planes. Avoid booking the last connecting flight of the day — missing it would mean an overnight stay.

☑ CONNECTING TO A REGIONAL CARRIER? Make sure smaller aircraft can accommodate your needs — especially if you use a power chair. If not, ask what alternate arrangements they'll provide.

Cruising With Wheelchairs

☑ BOOK EARLY. Accessible cabins may not be available in all price categories, and choices may be limited.

☑ Ask if the cruise line requires a DOCTOR'S CERTIFICATE. Do they require you to be accompanied by an ambulatory companion?

☑ Is your cabin's BATHROOM DOOR wide enough? Is there a step? Are all public restrooms accessible?

☑ Is there RAMPED ACCESS to all decks? Are all performance areas accessible?

Bus & Train Travel

☑ Amtrak requires at least 24-hours' and Greyhound requires at least 48-hours' notice **TO ARRANGE FOR ASSISTANCE** in stations and onboard trains. Reserve as far ahead as possible.

☑ Wheelchairs may be used within accessible sleeping accommodations and restrooms on Amtrak, however, capacity is limited. Accessible seating is also available in some coaches. **CALL AND ASK.**

☑ Standard-sized power wheelchairs may be transported on **AT LEAST ONE PASSENGER CAR** on most trains.

☑ If you require **THE SERVICES OF AN ASSISTANT,** Greyhound permits your companion to travel at no extra charge. Call and ask about requirements.

Lodging With Wheelchairs

☑ Most hotels now offer wheelchair-accessible rooms. **CALL THE HOTEL DIRECTLY** — not the national 800 number — and make sure their accommodations suit your particular needs.

☑ **DON'T ASSUME** that every new hotel is wheelchair accessible. Always ask specific questions.

☑ Make sure you will have EASY ACCESS to the hotel's entrance, elevators, public facilities, and to your room.

☑ SPECIFY TWO BEDS if you're traveling with an attendant.

Hearing-Impaired Travelers

☑ Be sure your hotel room has a fire alarm that FLASHES A LIGHT BRIGHT ENOUGH to wake you when you're sleeping.

☑ Airport terminals and airline reservation centers MUST HAVE TDD telephone devices.

Blind/Sight-Impaired Travelers

☑ Traveling with a SEEING-EYE DOG? Always inform the people who are booking your trip, so you can receive any services you need. Make sure the dog's harness is in good repair.

☑ TRY TO SIT AT WINDOW SEATS. They give you more room to store a cane, and if you travel with a seeing eye dog, it's easier for other passengers leaving certain seats. Sitting in the bulkhead of an airplane will give your guide dog more room to stretch out.

If complaining on the spot to the highest authority doesn't get results, go to 'Plan B.'

Pick the options most suited to your case.

Where & How

☑ If a problem is tangible, TAKE PHOTOS to document your complaint. Ask fellow travelers for their addresses and phone numbers if they'll help back you up.

☑ For action on complaints involving AIRPLANE SAFETY ISSUES, including airport security, child safety seats, hazardous materials, malfunctioning aircraft equipment or air-traffic procedures, call the Federal Aviation Administration: 1-800-FAA-SURE.

☑ If your COMPLAINT IS WITH AN AIRLINE, the Department of Transportation's Consumer Affairs Division can advise you of your rights under federal law and act as a mediator with the airline: (202) 366-2220.

☑ Contact the AMERICAN SOCIETY OF TRAVEL AGENTS, who may help mediate your complaint against a travel agency, airline, hotel or travel supplier. Write to: ASTA Consumer Affairs, 1101 King Street, Alexandria, VA 22314 or call (703) 739- 2782.

☑ If your TRAVEL AGENCY was involved, send a copy of your letter to them, and ask them to get involved on your behalf.

☑ Call your local BETTER BUSINESS BUREAU. And

check the state government listings in your phone book for any special offices dedicated to consumer affairs.

☑ Contact your local TV, radio or newspaper's **CONSUMER ACTION REPORTER** with your story. Try writing to the travel press.

☑ For information on filing a complaint for **VIOLATIONS OF THE AMERICANS WITH DISABILITIES ACT**, call (800) 514-0301 for voice, or (800) 514-0383 for TDD.

☑ For more information on **TELEMARKETING FRAUD OR TRAVEL SCAMS** — or to report one — call the National Fraud Information Center: (800) 876-7060.

☑ The U.S. Consumer Information Center offers **INFORMATIVE, LOW-COST BROCHURES** on travel safety, including the DOT's informative *Fly-Rights*. Write for their free Consumer Information Catalog: P.O. Box 100, Pueblo, CO 81002.

The Ultimate Packing Checklist

Scan this list and add your own entries, to build your sleekest, most complete travel bag.

Items with an open circle should be carried with you. Never put them in luggage that will be checked.

Must-Haves

- ○ Travelers checks
- ○ Credit cards
- ○ ATM card
- ○ Personal checks
- ○ Security wallet or moneybelt
- ○ Airline ticket
- ○ Travel itinerary
- ○ Confirmation numbers for all reservations
- ○ Travel insurance documentation
- ○ Personal address book
- ○ Personal medical summary
- ○ Medical alert card, tag or bracelet
- ○ Medical insurance card & claim forms
- ○ Eyeglasses, reading glasses and contact lenses
- ○ Mini-bottle of contact lens solution
- ○ Camera, film and lenses
- ○ Binoculars
- ○ Personal stereo and music
- ☐ Hunting/fishing licenses
- ☐ Luggage tags
- ☐ Travel alarm clock

- ☐ Flashlight, batteries and extra bulb
- ☐ Wouldn't-hurt-to-lose-it watch
- ☐ Travel guidebooks
- ☐ Up-to-date maps
- ☐ Pocket compass
- ☐ Extra batteries: camera, calculator, hearing aid
- ☐ Comfortable old walking shoes
- ☐ Running shoes or sneakers
- ☐ Sunglasses
- ☐ Folding umbrella
- ☐ Raincoat/poncho
- ☐ Paper and dependable pen
- ☐ Empty tote bag, for bringing back souvenirs
- ☐ Book or magazines
- ☐ Postage stamps and addresses

- ☐ _____
- ☐ _____
- ☐ _____
- ☐ _____
- ☐ _____

Carry Photocopies!

Guard these like the real documents.

- O Airline ticket, all pages
- O Passport, visa
- O Itinerary
- O All credit cards, fronts and backs
- O Travelers check numbers & refund instructions
- O Auto insurance policy and agent's phone number
- O Travel insurance documentation
- O Personal address book
- O Your eyeglass prescription
- O Personal health profile (page 216)
- O Medical insurance card & claims form
- O Phone numbers of trusted neighbor, family member, physician, dentist, optician and insurance agent
- O Your pet's health certificate and inoculation documentation

Copies For Trusted Friends

- ☐ Passport number
- ☐ Itinerary
- ☐ Auto insurance policy number and agent's phone number
- ☐ Travel insurance documentation
- ☐ Medical insurance card number
- ☐ Phone number of family member

Personal Packing

Pour liquids into plastic bottles. Tighten all screw-tops. Place bottles in zipper-lock bags.

- ○ All prescription medicines in original containers
- ☐ Aspirin/pain reliever
- ☐ Vitamins
- ☐ Allergy medication
- ☐ Travel hair drier
- ☐ Travel iron/steamer
- ☐ Curling iron
- ☐ Mini shoeshine kit
- ☐ Nail clipper/file
- ☐ Cotton swabs

- ☐ Moisturizer
- ☐ Razor blades
- ☐ Shaving cream
- ☐ Bath soap
- ☐ Lip balm
- ☐ Lipscreen
- ☐ Toothpaste, toothbrush, dental floss
- ☐ Mouthwash
- ☐ Comb, hairbrush
- ☐ Shampoo, conditioner
- ☐ Deodorant
- ☐ Perfume/cologne/aftershave
- ☐ Cosmetic kit
- ☐ Sanitary protection
- ☐ Dentures -- kit and cleanser
- ☐ Cold-water fabric wash
- ☐ Tissues
- ☐ Birth control
- ☐ Condoms, because these are the '90's
- ☐ _____
- ☐ _____

And Don't Forget...

- O Emergency smoke hood
- O Spare eyeglasses, reading glasses and contact lenses
- O Motion-sickness remedy
- O Chewing gum for ear-pressure relief
- O Eye drops
- O Antacids
- O Neck pillow
- ☐ Sunscreen — SPF 15 or higher
- ☐ Sunburn creme
- ☐ Cold/flu remedy
- ☐ Throat lozenges
- ☐ Anti-diarrhea medicine
- ☐ Laxative
- ☐ Athletes' foot remedy
- ☐ Sleeping pills
- ☐ Dandruff shampoo
- ☐ Bug repellant
- ☐ Adhesive tape & bandages
- ☐ Antiseptic ointment
- ☐ Moleskin
- ☐ Nasal spray/antihistamines

- ☐ Foam insoles
- ☐ Bathroom tissue
- ☐ Yeast infection treatment
- ☐ Disposable toilet seat covers
- ☐ Styptic pencil
- ☐ Saline nasal spray
- ☐ Shoehorn
- ☐ Small lint brush
- ☐ Spot remover
- ☐ Sleep shades
- ☐ Moist towelettes
- ☐ Rubber sink stopper
- ☐ Fly swatter
- ☐ Swimsuit & pool shoes
- ☐ Visor or brimmed hat
- ☐ Scarf

- ☐ _____
- ☐ _____
- ☐ _____
- ☐ _____

Feel More Secure With...

O Loud police whistle or shriek alarm
O Extra set of luggage keys
O Lead-lined film pouch
☐ Portable hotel door lock
☐ Water purification tablets

Fix Most Emergencies With...

☐ Duct tape
☐ Tweezers
☐ Safety pins, needle & thread
☐ Small first aid kit
☐ Eyeglass repair kit
☐ Snub-nosed scissors
☐ Extension cord
☐ Swiss Army knife
☐ Crazy Glue
☐ Clear nail polish
☐ Can and bottle opener
☐ All-in-one tool

Taking Care Of Business

- O Business cards
- O Personal calendar
- O Company checks
- O Mini-tape recorder
- O Laptop or notebook computer
- O Pocket-sized calculator
- O Phone/fax/extension numbers
- O Long distance calling card
- O Extra batteries and charger
- ☐ Overnight express shipping labels
- ☐ Small stapler with extra staples
- ☐ Pad of stick-on notes
- ☐ Extra letterhead and envelopes
- ☐ Stamps
- ☐ Breath mints
- ☐ Paper clips & rubber bands
- ☐ Pencils, pens, markers
- ☐ Scissors

- ☐ _____
- ☐ _____

If You're From Another Country

- O Passports/proof of citizenship
- O Passport holders
- O Visa
- O Inoculations and health or vaccination certificates
- O International driving permit
- O U.S. dollars and pocket change
- O English language phrase book
- O Conversion tables or pocket calculator
- ☐ Adapters for U.S. outlets

- O _____
- O _____

Flying

- O Airline tickets & seat reservations
- O Airline VIP card
- O Frequent flyer number, stickers or card
- O Inflatable neck pillow
- O Kids' busy bag
- O _____

Driving Supplies

- ☐ Extra set of car keys
- ☐ Driver's licenses for each driver
- ☐ Auto insurance policy number and insurance agent's phone number
- ☐ Owner's manual for car
- ☐ Auto club membership card
- ☐ Road flares & roadway reflectors
- ☐ White cloth to hang in emergencies
- ☐ First-aid kit and book
- ☐ CB radio or cellular phone
- ☐ Empty, approved fuel container
- ☐ Bottled drinking water
- ☐ Notepaper, pencil, tape
- ☐ Working flashlight, extra batteries and bulbs
- ☐ Up-to-date maps
- ☐ Litter bag
- ☐ Car snacks
- ☐ Games and toys for the kids
- ☐ Jumper cables
- ☐ Extra motor oil
- ☐ Extra antifreeze

- ☐ Extra windshield fluid
- ☐ Extra set of wiper blades
- ☐ Extra set of fuses
- ☐ Spare tire, jack & lug wrench
- ☐ Fire extinguisher
- ☐ Bungee cords
- ☐ Blankets and pillows
- ☐ Car window sunscreens
- ☐ Workgloves
- ☐ Warm clothes
- ☐ Rain gear
- ☐ Coins for tolls and emergencies
- ☐ Tissues, toilet paper, paper towels
- ☐ Resealable plastic bags
- ☐ Premoistened towelettes

WINTRY CLIMATES OR HIGH ALTITUDES

- ☐ Ice scraper/snow brush
- ☐ Snow tires, chains or traction mats
- ☐ Rock salt/sand/kitty litter
- ☐ Shovel
- ☐ Nonperishable high-energy foods
- ☐ Extra warm clothes and blankets
- ☐ Red cloth to hang in emergencies

Emergency Health Profile

*Photocopy these two pages; put one
in your wallet and one in your carry-on.*

Name _____

Home phone (   ) _____

In An Emergency

Doctor _____

Phone (   ) _____

Health Insurer _____

Policy number _____

For medical authorization (   ) _____

I suffer from _____

_____

I'm allergic to _____

_____

Medications I take _____

_____

In An Emergency, Please Call

Name _____

Phone (___ **)** _____

I wear contact lenses ☐ Yes ☐ No

Blood Type _____

Last tetanus shot _____

Dentist _____

   Phone (___) _____

Eye doctor _____

   Phone (___) _____

Other Doctor _____

   Phone (___) _____

Neighbor/Relative _____

   Phone (___) _____

Attorney _____

   Phone (___) _____

Air Travel Itinerary

*Photocopy these two pages;
bring one in your carry-on and leave one
with a family member, colleague or neighbor.*

Name _____

Home phone ( ) _____

Departure

Date _____Time _____

City/Airport _____

Airline _____ Flight _____

Connecting flight number _____

Leaves _____ ☐ am ☐ pm

Final arrival _____ ☐ am ☐ pm

Staying At

Place _____

Address _____

Phone ( ) _____

Fax ( ) _____

Returning

Date_____ Time _____

City/Airport _____

Airline _____ Flight _____

Connecting flight number _____

Leaves _____ ☐ am ☐ pm

Final arrival _____☐ am ☐ pm

Important Numbers

Airline Ticket Serial Number _____

Travel Agent _____

   Phone (   ) _____

Airline _____

   Phone (   ) _____

Car Rental Agency _____

   Phone (   ) _____

Car/Shuttle Service _____

   Phone (   ) _____

Pre-Trip Car Checklist

An ounce of prevention is worth two tons of cure.

☐ **OIL AND FILTER**

☐ **BRAKES**

☐ **BATTERY:** fluid level on batteries with filler caps.

☐ **AIR FILTER:** shake clean or replace.

☐ **WIPER BLADES:** wipe clean or replace.

☐ **TIRES:** look for bulges, nicks and uneven tread wear. Check spare tire. Check air pressure while tires are cool.

☐ **COOLING SYSTEM** and coolant levels: never open the radiator cap of a heated engine.

☐ **HOSES:** with the engine off, look for leaks, bulges and soft spots

☐ **BELTS:** with the engine off, roll each belt between your thumb and forefinger, looking on all sides for splits, cracks or grease spots. Modern belts frequently don't show wear — follow the manufacturer's recommended replacement schedule. The correct tension should be about one-half inch of give.

☐ **LIGHTS:** emergency flashers, headlights, turn signals, brake lights, tail lights and interior lights. Make sure the headlights are properly aimed.

☐ **SEATBELTS:** check belts and retractor mechanisms for signs of wear, especially if the car has been in an accident. Replace if necessary.

☐ **GLASS:** clean your windshield inside and out, and wipe off mirrors and headlights.

☐ **AUTO CLUB MEMBERSHIP CARD**

☑ **FOR EMERGENCIES, BRING:**

☐ jumper cables
☐ extra motor oil
☐ extra antifreeze
☐ windshield fluid
☐ working spare tire
☐ tire jack
☐ lug wrench
☐ work gloves
☐ clean rags
☐ paper towels
☐ warm blanket
☐ extra clothes
☐ working flashlight

☐ extra flashlight batteries
☐ several road flares
☐ roadway reflectors
☐ can of flat fixer
☐ white cloth
☐ red cloth (in winter)
☐ coins for tolls
☐ first-aid kit
☐ ice scraper
☐ snow brush
☐ traction mats
☐ salt/sand/kitty litter
☐ shovel

Share
Your
Wisdom!

USA

If your travels have taught you tips not included here, mail them to us.

If your tip is included in a later edition, we will send you a free book from the CorkScrew Press catalog, as thanks.

Send your tips to:
CorkScrew Press
4470-107 Sunset Blvd., Suite 234
Los Angeles, CA 90027

Nobody expects you to use all these safety tips.

But the ones you DO use could make all the difference.